CAGED

MEMOIRES OF A POLICE CONSTABLE 2005 – 2013

BY ANDREW RUDD

This Book is dedicated to my wife Claire, who is the most wonderful woman, my best friend and inspiration in life. Also, to my Daughters Alison and Jessica and Step Daughter Olivia. You are all my reason for existing, and I hope that one day you will read this book and be proud of your daddy. I love you all more than cheese!

INTRODUCTION

My name is Andrew Rudd, and up until Friday the 14th June 2013 I was a serving Police officer. The reasons I am no longer a police officer are detailed within this work, along with many stories, observations and accounts of both my work and that of others.

The events that are outlined in this book are all real life. They all happened and the accounts I have provided are as accurate as I can make them. The names have been changed to protect others privacy as have some of the locations and other details that would draw attention directly to those involved.

In writing this book, it is my intention to show those outside of the police service the atmosphere in which police officers work, the incidents and events they become involved in, and the effect they can have on the person underneath the uniform. There are many television programmes based in fact and fiction that show the day to day duties of a police officer, and I have even appeared in one such fly on the wall documentary. However these do not show the complete picture for many different reasons, and although they provide an entertaining insight into the world of policing in the UK they sadly fall short of telling the full story; what happens behind the scenes and the interplay between the many personalities and characters involved in this world both inside and outside the law.

So, read on. It is my aim to show you the reader some of the things that make the British Police Force the best in the world, and also some of the things that make it not so good. You will read things that you may find disturbing, shocking or that may anger or upset you. However, at the end you will have a valid insight, supplied by someone who has done the job, and has provided an objective view. I will also provide an insight into a sufferer of Post-Traumatic Stress disorder which almost destroyed my life and did destroy my career. I want to draw attention to this illness, and the fact that it is more common among Police Officers than you may think. People think that PTSD is an illness suffered by Military personnel only. I want to explode that myth and show what it is like to have PTSD and increase awareness of this debilitating and devastating condition.

I hope that you enjoy this experience and gain something from it.

Cheers

Andrew Rudd

CHAPTER 1 – THE BEGINNING

I joined the police force on the 30th August 2005. I was not a stranger to the service as I had for the proceeding five years been working as a control room operator in the Force Control Room. This was a great job; on the end of the radio to officers out there on the streets I "Dispatched" resources to incidents and managed them to their conclusion. I also answered 999 calls from the public and dealt with thousands of incidents over five years, and every day was different. But after each day I gained more of a sense that the real job was so much more and wanted to try it. At the age of 30 I decided that it was now or never and applied.

I turned up on my first day as a police officer in a suit, desperate to be issued the uniform. We were welcomed and issued with our uniforms which took most of the day (there were 24 of us) and given the start of an induction to the Constabulary. That night I took the significant amount of kit I had been issued home and spent hours pressing shirts, trousers and polishing my boots. I could not stop looking at it and spent all night in bed gazing at it hung up on the wardrobe door. I was so proud that I would be wearing it the following day, and so excited at what lay ahead; which was two more weeks at HQ doing an induction before twelve weeks away at the Police Training centre, in Ryton upon Dunsmore (Near Coventry) learning the trade proper. Two days later I stood with my new colleagues and swore my oath as a Police Officer - the proudest moment of my life, outside of the birth of my kids. From that point I had all the powers and responsibilities as a Constable and was as proud as punch. I remember the Deputy Chief Constable gave a speech, during which he said, "you have extraordinary powers as Police Officers now, and in return the public expects extraordinary standards of behaviour from you". I took this to heart and used it as my mantra in the years to follow. My new warrant card burned a hole in my pocket and I was so keen to flash it at the slightest excuse!

The next two weeks passed very quickly, learning about the Force and beginning to realise just what it meant to be a Police Officer and the restrictions that this placed on my private life. These were many, and although they were restrictive, I felt they were a fair price to pay and reasonable considering the responsibility that I would now have. For instance, I could no longer hold any public office or join the Various political groups, including the BNP (In which I had no interest anyway). The place at which I lived had to be approved by the Force and when moving home I had to ask permission first, if the job said no, then I could not live there- simple.

I had to be conscious at all times of what I did whilst off duty and make sure that none of my actions could reflect badly on the force or on the office of Constable. The old saying 'A police officer is never off duty' I found to be absolutely true. I found that I was expected, off duty to intervene if I saw a crime taking place, or step in; in certain situations, to protect the public or keep the peace. This had knock on effects; a night out with my friends was no longer a congenial night of drinking until I fell over! I had to restrain myself and stay in control just in case anything happened (and it did several times over my career). As a police officer the power of arrest extends to being on or off duty anywhere in England and Wales (Including British Registered Flights when flying abroad). Failure to act reasonably to intervene or make myself known as a police officer could be seen as a dereliction of duty leading to dismissal. This is a serious issue and is not to be taken lightly and understandably there is an expectation that the person bestowed with this power would exercise exceptional standards of behaviour whilst off duty. I aimed to embrace it whole heartedly.

The result of this was that the number of friends I had diminished markedly. I was and always have been a law abiding and honest person (and so I should be) but some of my friends were less so. I am not talking about them being hardened criminals or robbers, but some may have enjoyed a bit of weed now and again and others may download the odd illegal film or take cocaine over the weekend. Other than dabble with recreational drugs in my late teens and early twenties I did not touch drugs and never have since, so I was apart from this. But some people, at the edge of my circle of friends melted away. I had made it clear that my new job meant I could not be subjected to things such as drugs, or petty crime and I either broke contact with, or had it broken off for me by several acquaintances. Others who were perfectly law abiding and honest people decided that they did not want to know me anymore as they just did not like coppers; this was fine with me and I was happy with the choices I made. I still am. Some see this as being an unacceptable price to pay for just doing a job but for me it was necessary, and above all the right thing to do. I wanted to be a police officer above all else.

A brief example was one night when I had gone out with a mate for a quiet drink. I had known this person for many years, and we were close friends, I respected him and he me, or so I thought. However, we had a few drinks and he had driven to the pub. I was walking home but he had other ideas and offered me a lift in his car. I said to him something along the lines of "What, you can't be fucking serious? You know what I do" and his reply was along the lines of "What use is there being the mate of a copper if there are no fringe benefits". I told him, in no uncertain terms that I would not be getting in his car, and that he would not be either. This was met with the challenge "What are you going to do to stop me"? to which I replied, "I will arrest you". This person is no longer a friend. The fact that he thought my being a copper meant he could do what he liked around me, because of our friendship told me he was

no friend of mine anyway. It was no loss. I do not think I have set eyes on the bloke

since, but even now I am outside the job I would still ignore him.

CHAPTER 2 – TRAINING SCHOOL

Three weeks into my service I went off to the Police training School at Ryton on Dunsmore, near Coventry in the Midlands. The training went on from Monday to Friday with us all arriving Sunday evening and departing back home mid-afternoon on the Friday. I arrived and was allocated a room in one of the billets that were almost identical to the barrack blocks you will find on military bases all over the world. I had a small room, with a drop leaf table about 18 inches across that served as a desk as well as a sink and wardrobe. The bed was tiny but serviceable. All in all, it was not the kind of thing I was used to, having come from a nice home that contained my wife and kids but I accepted it. After all it was only for three months. However, as the building filled up with officers from all over the country I began to hear the odd voice of dissension, both male and female. There were several 'princesses' both male and female who did not want to live in these conditions with no creature comforts. I was surprised to find that the block would hold male and female police officers who shared all the toilet facilities and showers; so I could understand some of the protests but again I was OK with it (as a bloke I supposed I would be). I unpacked and went down to explore, finding the bar. There was anything up to 400 officers at the centre from all over the country, so a bar had been in existence for many years. The alcohol was cheap, not so cheap as you would find in a mess on a military camp but probably around half of that you would pay in a pub. I found this strange. All the warnings I had back at HQ regarding alcohol and its potential dangers and here I was at the police training centre with a bar with half price booze! For some of the younger officers (I was 31 and happily married at the time) this was magna from heaven and many were already boozing lustily! For me things were different. I enjoyed a drink as much as anyone, but I was on a budget, £20 a week from home as that was all I could afford. I had a mortgage, and a wife and kids to look after. However, the bar turned out to be a nice place to relax after a hard day and was a meeting area for all of us to unwind and discuss the training. It also became a place where barriers were let down, (sometimes too much), but more on this at a later point.

The course started and it was bizarre. At the beginning of each lesson one of the tutors would ask "is there anyone in the room who is an investigative journalist?" and "No recording devices are allowed in this lesson". I found out the reason for this was a documentary broadcast on television called the "secret policeman" where a journalist joined the police force and secretly filmed his experiences in another training centre (Hendon). The resulting programme made numerous accusations of racism within the police service which followed hot on the heels of the McPherson report into the tragic death of Steven Lawrence, and the resultant branding of the Met as being 'institutionally racist'. The documentary served only to feed the fire and the Police Force was running scared of making things worse and feeding the perception that the Police Force was institutionally Racist.

The weeks went by and I learned. I learned the law and my place in it, as well as how to defend myself, make arrests and use force on people. The practical training, I undertook to be honest was not really great, due to unrealistic nature of it. I had an expectation that if I were to be trained to defend myself or protect others in a situation that could result in death I would be trained in a realistic manner. However, it seemed that the organisation was so hell bent on preventing injuries any actual realism disappeared. It was all very gentle, and all risk was removed. We did learn various methods to take aggressive persons to the ground, various holds based on pain compliance as well as 'crisis communications' where you would have to hand cuff and arrest someone who was non-compliant and resisting. But there was no edge to any of it, and there was always an air of friendliness, which robbed what little realism existed. Having said this, I left the course knowing various holds and techniques and how to use and apply my handcuffs. There was no training in the use of my baton or incapacitant spray (which was done later in force). Much of what a police officer can do is based upon pain compliance. We were taught various holds and methods in which to take a non-compliant person to the floor, and how to apply handcuffs to him or her. However, this was never done in a real situation, in that we always buddied up with a colleague and threw each other around a bit. If it hurt too much the other person tapped on the ground and you got up. I had expected angry man and role actors; upping the ante and trying to intimidate me but this never happened. In addition in the weekly consolidation role plays, during which we were expected to display our knowledge and make arrests we had to perform 'touch arrests' which meant as soon as I took someone by the arm and told them they were under arrest there was no struggling allowed!. Well that prepared me for the real world…. NOT!

This was a theme that continued back with my home force (who at one point did everything it could to remove the use of any force from its training on the orders of the chief constable). We had several sessions of personal defence training after the course, and when I finally went out into the real world I knew the theory and practical aspects of personal safety training up to a point, but I did not feel confident in applying it in the real world. I was apprehensive and worried.

Academically I did well. I absorbed the information given to me and passed all the exams as they came. Again, I was surprised to see people failing exam after exam but nothing really happening to them. It was plain that some people needed more help and support to get through, but once it was apparent that the knowledge was not sinking in there was no action to address this that I was aware of. The result was that people were passing the course and returning to their home forces, almost ready to go out and meet the public without the required level of law knowledge.

I left Ryton after 12 weeks with little ceremony. The passing out parade had historically been a major part of the course with family and friends coming to see their loved ones parading as police officers for the first time. However, this practice had been stopped years before. We had a dining in night which was a nice night where we all hired suits and bow ties and relaxed at the end of the course over a meal and a few drinks, but this same function was the reason that there would be no parade, or that wives, parents, boyfriends etc were no longer invited. I should explain..

I soon realised that the whole course was a shag fest. There were people at it everywhere! At one point I was lying in my bed reading a book with both neighbours at it, the one across the corridor and above me on the floor above. At this point I have to say that this is not a criticism, in that there were a lot of young people in their late teens or early twenties, and with a cheap bar and plenty of the opposite sex about nature will take its course. But…. A lot of these people had partners, boyfriends, husbands or wives at home, and they were playing away. It turned out that the local police had been called to dining in nights in the past as partners and spouses were turning up and discovering what their loved ones had been up to! There were fights, arrests, and officers kicked out of the job. Twelve weeks of training and kicked out on the last day for stuff you have been up to behind the wife's back! The bosses had a choice, stop all the shagging, or stop passing out parades. The parade went, as it was the cheaper option and the sex continued. Wonderful, I was deprived of a proud moment due to the inability of some to keep it in their pants.

There was one story of note during my training. I had a mate from my home force that I buddied up with. We would meet up in the bar after class, play badminton or just study together. After the classes were over it could be a very solitary existence and we enjoyed each other's company. However, the behaviour of my mate (for the sake of argument I will call him Steve) began to disturb me. His behaviour towards one member of our group who was female began to bother me. He would make sexual comments and touch her inappropriately, patting her bottom or putting his arm around her. His language was sexually explicit also, nothing you would not expect to hear in a pub or football ground but in these surroundings with everyone on high alert for anything sexist, racist or homophobic it was stupid, and I told him so. It came to a head one night in the bar. He came over to join me and a group of my classmates who were having a drink. One of those, Pete, was openly gay. He was a nice fellow and we worked together in our personal safety training, throwing each other to the ground and applying handcuffs to each other. We had a certain amount of banter between us that came from our friendship as grown men who had no fears about each other's sexuality. I would call him an old queen and he would call me similar names based on my heterosexuality. However, this did not happen in a group, only when we were egging each other on in the gym and certainly never in the bar! The conversation (as it often does when you are drinking) came around to partners and sex. Pete mentioned a friend of his whom he had split up with recently and as he said the guy's name Steve's ears seemed to prick up. "Are you a fucking poof then?" he asked forcefully. When Pete confirmed that he was indeed gay, and asked what that had to do with anything, he was met with homophobic abuse including "I had better keep my back to the wall when you are around from now on" and other choice remarks I do not wish to dignify with space here. Pete to his credit did not say anything and later told me he would not rise to such ignorance. I was however offended, as were others in the group I was wondering how to proceed when it came to light that Steve's comments had been overheard by the next table, upon which sat the chair of the gay association of the British police. Wheels were set in motion.

For the first time I witnessed the machine known as 'Professional Standards' in action. They really went to work. A team led by a Detective Chief inspector came from our home force and spent the rest of the week investigation the matter, along with several other incidents that came to light. I was told to give a statement (which I did willingly even though I was not told I had a choice) and Steve did not appear the following week. I was told he had been called in to see the Deputy Chief Constable (DCC) and been told in no uncertain terms to either resign, or be dismissed with the prospect of the force suing him for reimbursement of uniform and training received so far.

What struck me was the thorough nature in with PSD went after Steve. I agree that what he had said and done up to that point was disgusting and meant he had no place in the police service, but I was taken aback by the savage nature of it all. I later saw the same savagery aimed at other colleagues for whom it was unfounded and eventually myself, but that is for later.

CHAPTER 3 – SHIFT

I had finished my initial training. I was about to go out and face the public as a police officer for the first time whether I felt I was ready or not. To be honest I felt ready. I knew that the training was not the end and I would spend every day learning for the rest of my career but I felt equipped to do the job. I was posted to Huntingdon Police Station at first, to spend ten weeks with a tutor constable who would continue my training. During the ten weeks I had to complete a PDP (personal development portfolio) to evidence the fact that I was competent to achieve independent patrol status (allowed to go out on my own).

On my first day I met my tutor, an experienced officer called Wendy. Wendy was a lovely girl, in her mid to late twenties who was very pretty and very chatty. She got a lot of male attention and not just from her colleagues. She worked with another Constable, called Geoff who was vastly experienced and had transferred from the Met, and had a Met attitude. I don't mean anything bad by this, but he did see himself as being a law mogul and far more streetwise that the officers in our area, who were seen as country bumpkins! That said he was a nice guy and was always helpful. I met the rest of my shift, who included someone who I would develop a close personal friendship that endures to this day. Pasty as he is known (because of his Cornish origins as well as his home baking skills) was new to the job too, having just gone independent. He was a miserable and cantankerous old git from a military background, but he was committed completely to doing the job right. I connected with him immediately and we got on from day one.

Day one then. Police officers on joining and going out for the first time are looking for two major milestones. Obviously that first arrest is always at the front of your mind, and secondly dealing with your first sudden death. Depending on what way you want to look at it, I was lucky or unlucky enough to get these things done almost straight away.

My first arrest was a chap known as Scouse Walsh. He was aptly named as he was from Liverpool as well as having the second name Walsh. I was to find that many of our 'customers' would have similar nicknames or street names either bestowed upon them by the police, or their criminal peers. I was in the station with Wendy and Geoff (mid-way through my first day) when the message came over the radio. A shoplifting had taken place and the offenders had been seen getting into a red car which had driven out onto the ring road. The police station happened to be on the ring road and the car (known to Wendy and Geoff anyway) would have to pass the police station. We shot out into the car (with me in the back of course) and got out onto the ring road. Another mobile had seen the offending car and was following it, very considerately waiting for us before he stopped it so that I could get my first arrest. I was sweating buckets in the car as we made our way to where my colleague was stopping the vehicle (getting my first taste of a blue light run). Wendy was giving me advice, making sure I understood what the arrest was for and telling me about Walsh in general. He was a heroin addict, and had several contagious bloods borne diseases such as hepatitis and it was rumoured HIV. He was also a big guy and could be a handful when he wanted to be, as could his girlfriend who was with him.

I was shitting myself. More due to the fact that I might forget the caution or screw it up in another manner that would cause me to look stupid than any harm that may come to me. The drive was only about a mile, but it seemed like ten despite

Wendy treating me to my first blue light run. We did however arrive to see that a colleague had stopped the car and was talking to Walsh. We joined them and Wendy looked to me and nodded, encouraging me. I managed to look at Walsh and tell him he was under arrest and got the caution out ok. However, Walsh did not want to get out of the car, saying his leg hurt. I learned later that this was not the case, but small things like this can inspire terror into an officer part way through his first arrest. Walsh was not to know this of course, and this was not his first time (as it were) so he knew the ropes far better than I did. He was on bail, so the likely outcome was that he would be remanded in custody after this arrest. He had just stolen in order to pay for heroin so his need for it was quite severe, if he could get himself taken to hospital there would be a delay in getting to custody and he would get some methadone which would of at least stopped his pain. Now with my newly trained human rights head my first thought was to get an ambulance to check this guy over. However, I was now in the real world (as reminded by Wendy and Geoff) and their attitude was slightly different. "Come on, out of the car Scouse or we will get you out" Geoff intoned in his cockney accented voice. And he looked at me as if to say, "come on mate, time to get stuck in!" Walsh did not say anything but did not get out of the car either. We were standing next to him in the driver's seat and he had the door open. I was stood in the gap between where Walsh was sitting and the door. I said to Walsh "Please get out of the car sir, you are under arrest and need to come with me" in as calm a voice as I could muster (as inside I was shitting myself). Walsh did not move. I saw that he had his hands on the wheel and after another moment of looking uncertainly at Wendy and getting the same 'get on with it' look I quickly put a cuff on Walsh's wrist and looked at him as if to say "last chance mate". There was still no movement, so I pulled Walsh from the car (amid much wailing from his girlfriend). He did not resist, or help remaining a dead weight; he was completely passive (what we were trained to call passive resistance) so it took a lot of effort to get him out of the car. Once out of the car I applied the other handcuff to his other wrist and suddenly he was up on his feet. He walked calmly to the van and allowed me to open the door. He then got in. He did not say a word. Relief was flooding through my mind that I had done it correctly, although Wendy later said I waited too long, but that would come with experience. The job was not yet over. I had to attend the strangely named Custody 'suite' and book him into police custody, giving the custody sergeant a verbal account of why Walsh had been arrested so they could authorise or decline his detention at the police station. I was really nervous, and I remember the custody Sergeant talking me through it which was really kind. After this the shop had to be visited and a statement obtained regarding the theft from the witness, and confirmation that they wanted to press charges.

This was obviously my first time booking a prisoner in, and Wendy walked me through it all. It was tough, particularly relating the circumstances of the arrest to the custody sergeant, who kindly gave me a couple of prompts. In addition to this as the arresting officer I had to search the detainee, to make sure that he had no implements in his possession that he could use to injure himself or others. This is vitally important for the care of the detainee and more importantly to me, to cover my own arse in case something went wrong. It is a part of the job I hated doing but I did it well enough, apologetically patting Walsh down and searching his person in as detailed manner as possible. That done I took him to the documentation room and took his fingerprints (a messy job as we were still in the age of using ink) and his photograph. We did not need his DNA as it was already on the database. This done I locked him away in a cell while we went to complete our enquiries. Walsh barely said a word throughout but did tell the custody sergeant he was suffering from depression and had suicidal thoughts as well as a heroin dependency. His cell had a permanent CCTV feed, so he was watched at all times, and was visited in his cell at least once every thirty minutes by the custody staff.

This done; we had to prepare to interview Walsh, and to do this we needed to gather the evidence that tied him to the theft. Wendy and I went to the shop involved and the security staff there had helpfully completed their statement (they had a lot of practice)! And provided the CCTV on a disc. Armed thus we made our way back to the station to interview Walsh under caution for the offence. Walsh had a habit of admitting all his crimes at the first opportunity, so we anticipated an easy time. This was not what we got, however. On entering the Custody Suite (or cell block as we called it) I was immediately struck by a persistent and repetitive dull thud coming from the cells every five seconds or so. It was the kind of noise I could only describe as 'meaty', the kind of noise you get when you are hitting a steak with a meat tenderiser. It did not bode well for whoever was making the sound but a sickening sensation in the pit of my stomach told me it was Walsh. A quick chat with the custody officer confirmed this. Walsh had for the past 30 minutes or so been lying face up on his bed and repeatedly smashing the back of his head against the brick wall. He was not talking to anyone or asking for anything. A doctor had been called to assess his mental state, but his ETA was another hour away. Until then we could not interview him, as until a doctor had examined him, we could not tell if he was fit to be interviewed. At this point my virginal policing mind was thinking about why Walsh could be in his cell doing this to himself with no one stopping him? Of course by then I was inexperienced and had not had the time to become cynical or used to the daily goings on in a Police Custody Suite so I did not question what was happening, but I was asked while I was there to go and speak to Walsh and tell him what was happening. I went to his cell and looked in the observation hatch before opening the door. Sure enough Walsh was lying on his bed, smacking his head with a lot of force into the wall. The back of his head was bleeding and there was a bright red stain on the wall as he continued. I asked him why he was doing what he did, and without pausing he told me "Its to cover up the pain". He was clucking, what we called cold turkey, the illness felt when withdrawing from Heroin. It must have been terrible for him to be in so much physical pain for the want of smack he would rather smash the back of his head in, but at the same time I did not feel too much sympathy as at the end of the day he was a criminal who had got himself hooked on drugs, no one else.

We never did get to interview Walsh as our shift ended before the doctor arrived and he was dealt with by the oncoming shift. I found out the next day that he had indeed been remanded after being prescribed some methadone and ended up being sent to prison for a variety of offences. What was, in a way funny about the whole thing was that the prison sentence effectively saved his life. He was suffering from a form of blood poisoning that would have proved fatal had he continued in the lifestyle he was in before I arrested him. With the stable (but not necessarily drug free) prison environment his condition was discovered and brought under control so his life was saved. I would love to say that this prompted him to get off heroin and take the second chance that had been given him, but after his release I came into contact with Walsh many times and not for good reasons. From what I recall he is now back in prison having committed a very serious assault that got him a very long sentence, and to be honest that is where he belongs.

I got to the second week with Wendy. The first week and the beginning of the second had been a steep learning curve. I had made several arrests and was getting more comfortable but still lacked confidence in my knowledge and ability. Wendy had mentioned sudden deaths and given me a prep talk but at that point none had come in while I was on duty for the area. People often ask why the police have to be involved in certain circumstances when someone dies, more often than not at home. The shortest answer is that when someone passes away, a death certificate has to be issued detailing the cause of death before the death can be registered and a funeral arranged. When someone has died from a protracted illness such as cancer or the death is expected then the person's GP will normally issue a death certificate and the police do not need to become involved at all. However death as in life, does not conform to making things easy so many people die suddenly, for various reasons that could be at home or in public places. In times such as these, police are needed to investigate the death and complete a report to the coroner who will then oversee the rest of the investigation, arrange a post mortem examination and ultimately issue a death certificate and in the case of suspicious deaths or suicide preside over an inquest.

So when the call went out over the radio about a 26 year old male, in cardiac arrest at his home Wendy immediately called up and took the job on. We blue lit to the scene, and on our arrival we found an ambulance (the ambulance service had called us in). The paramedic met us at the door and told us that the man was deceased, and had been for some hours. It was around 1100 in the morning and the body was still in bed. The paramedic had already completed his report and was soon off on his way to his next job. Wendy and I were left at the scene. Inside the house were the deceased person's father and his younger sister. As you can imagine they were absolutely in pieces and both were completely broken. I was not used to such situations at all and was at a loss as to what to say or do, apart from mumble my sincerest condolences and try and offer some comfort. I explained why we were there and explained that we would have to see the deceased and speak a little about his life, and any illness he had suffered from. The father stated that his wife was at work and was on her way home, but at that time did not know their son was dead. Tommy was 26 years old and six weeks previously had been as fit and well as it was possible to be. However it had all ended one day during a game of football. He suffered a sudden and unexpected heart attack, which the doctors could not explain, and none of the tests they had done had identified anything wrong. Tommy was said to have made a full recovery and although had to take it easy the heart attack was said to have been completely random and there was no cause for concern that it would happen again. So for this to happen was a complete shock, made worse by the obvious pain and worry the family had been through six weeks previously.

Dad showed me up to Tommy's room. The door was closed and his father quickly retired downstairs, possibly not wanting to face the reality of seeing his dead son again without his wife present. Wendy looked at me, and just said "Are you ready", I nodded. She opened the door and we went in.

I had never seen a dead person before. Since that day I have seen dozens of dead people, in a variety of situations but I will never forget this one. It remains even now burned into my memory. The first thing that struck me was a distinctive odour. It was not particularly strong or bad but I found that this smell accompanied every deceased person I ever came into contact with, I cannot describe it other than I felt a faint sense of decay, but it was there and something I had never experienced before.

Tommy was in bed, and the paramedic had covered him. Fortunately he was wearing underwear so when we uncovered him there was no cause for Wendy to feel uncomfortable (more for Tommy's dignity than her own). I can't explain what he looked like, obviously the human form is very distinctive and recognisable but Tommy looked like he was made of porcelain, his skin was pale white with no colour, apart from at the bottom of his body which was red. I learned that when the heart stops the blood pools because of gravity and sinks to the lower parts of the anatomy. His expression was peaceful and blank; to my mind he had died in his sleep and felt no pain at all. However we needed to investigate the scene so with gloves on I searched his body. A macabre thing to have to do but we had to satisfy ourselves that at first look there was nothing suspicious about the death. I carefully looked Tommy over to check for any injuries at all, or sign of drug misuse or other unexplained articles. This also involved physically turning him over and checking his back. This was hard firstly, as he was heavy (but not overweight) but also, as he still felt warm (the duvet had kept the body temperature high). Most of all rigor mortis had set in and the body was incredibly stiff, like his joints had all turned to pipe cleaners.

After this search and a search of the room we found nothing suspicious and went back downstairs (after re-covering the body). We sat in the living room and I completed the paperwork with Tommy's dad. Pretty basic questions such as personal details, recent medical history and more awkward ones such as enquiring about his mental health or any previous attempts at suicide or self-harm. Thankfully I managed to get this done before his mother returned home and had also arranged for the undertaker to attend. His mum as you can imagine feared the worst but when Wendy confirmed it to her she was truly hysterical. The image of her throwing herself into Wendy's arms while she cried will never leave me. I do not think I have ever seen a human being in so much suffering and it was a massive struggle for us both not to give in and break up ourselves. What was most difficult was that she could not accept that he was dead. She went upstairs (and we had to follow) and before we could stop her got into bed with her son. Strictly speaking this was not allowed but as we were certain in our minds that death was from natural causes we did not insist she leave him. She cuddled up to him begging him to wake up and insisted he was just asleep, as he was still warm. It made no sense to contradict her at that time, and eventually her husband managed to coax her downstairs. However when he told her that the undertaker had been arranged she insisted her son would not be going anywhere and would wake up soon. Wendy was great; she had so much empathy and sympathy for the family. I took it in as much as I could, kept calm, answered questions and stayed professional but it was very hard to do in the circumstances. At one point I wondered if I had done the right thing becoming a police officer. Seeing that poor lady collapse into Wendy's arms was probably the most heart-breaking thing I have and will ever experience.

The mother was understandably very unpredictable and this was heightened yet again when the undertakers arrived to take the body to the mortuary. She refused to let the body leave the house. This posed a serious problem in that as this was a coroners case we had a responsibility to ensure the body reached the mortuary and there was a clear chain showing that there was no chance of the body being tampered with after our arrival. In effect the body was in police custody and we had to safely remove it from the house and escort it to the mortuary where its possession would be taken over by the hospital.

In the end the father, bless him coaxed his distraught wife into the living room and along with the undertakers we 'sneaked' the body downstairs and out of the house. If it was not such a harrowing situation it would have been funny and the stuff of many a laugh, as it was it was tragic and will stay with me forever.

For continuity we followed the funeral directors to the morgue and witnessed the body being handed over to the mortician. There was paperwork and receipts issued and our job was done. However as we stood in the mortuary the mortician started to take the deceased out of the body bag so that his body could be stored. I looked up and saw the mortician apparently wrestling with the body, as if he was trying to sit up. I practically shit myself, thinking that the guy was still alive. Had a miracle actually happened? No. As I outlined earlier the body had rigor mortis and the undertakers had to force the joints to straighten the arms and legs before it would fit in the bag. What I was seeing was the arms and legs trying to return to the foetal position that poor Tommy was in when he died which gave the impression that the body was actually moving of its own accord. I had never seen anything like it and hope not to see it again, the guy sat up and his arms began moving, terrible. I will tell you now… it made Shaun of the dead look very tame indeed. But all joking aside, I saw Tommy's face every time I closed my eyes at night for months afterwards.

I finished my tutor period with Wendy and never worked with her again. I was moved to another area. We bumped into each other from time to time and got on well. However I found a year or so later that Wendy had been dismissed from the service. I never found out exactly why but was told that she had been seen using drugs (cocaine) on a night out and had been asked to provide a sample for testing. I don't know whether she refused or failed but she was out on her ear soon afterwards. She was a good copper and I mused just how easy it was sack a copper, and it did not matter how good an officer they were.

CHAPTER 4 – FIRST JOB

After ten weeks of working with Wendy I was deemed competent and ready for independent patrol status. I arrived at my first posting at March Police Station. March is a small Fenland town near Peterborough and was also the place I grew up and lived with my wife and Children. As a brand new officer I could not yet drive police cars. It was too soon for me to be trained as a response driver and no one had arranged for me to do my test to drive police cars in normal conditions (i.e. no blue lights). This at the time was known as a grade 5 or basic permit. I arrived for my first shift and met my Sergeant, someone who I would work with often during my career. Chris was and is a brilliant copper. He is of a diminutive size and was younger than me (about 24 at the time) but had the heart of a lion and was very brave, knowledgeable and supportive. Anyhow I reported to him and quickly found myself out on foot patrol, something I was looking forward to and something I aimed to do as much as possible. However it had only been about 30 minutes when the control room radioed me and asked me to attend an incident, my first on my own and I have never been to a stranger incident since!

There was an escaped Ostrich. Do you have to read that again? Yes, an Ostrich. I am not kidding this is 100% true! An escaped, angry, scared male Ostrich. A local farmer had a small side-line keeping these creatures for their meat, which for a time was quite fashionable. I got in a car with Chris and we went out looking for this beast.

Now this was potentially a serious incident. The ostrich has a reputation for being somewhat of a birdbrain (pardon the pun) who stands still with its head in the sand. However a male Ostrich is a different matter. They can go from standing to 40 miles per hour in a few strides and can kick so hard they can break bones, or do very serious harm in any case. This was the half term school holidays and there were plenty of kids about enjoying the last of the fine weather before winter. It was a definite worry even though the fugitive bird was outside of town in fields.

We got to the general area and met the farmer. He confirmed that the thing was potentially dangerous and expressed his doubts that we would be able to catch it safely. He did however have a lot of experience with handling these animals and said if we could get it cornered he would get a rope around his neck and cover its head so he could get it into a horse box and back to his farm. This was no easy task. We were in open farmland which was completely flat and featureless apart from the old course of the river Nene which flowed about half a mile to the north of us. One problem was that the land the Ostrich was on was next to the A141, which is a major road in Fenland and one of the busiest routes. If the Ostrich had got on there it would have panicked and any resulting collision with a vehicle may have proved fatal to all parties involved.

We could see the bird. It was about 100 metres away from us in a field heading towards the river. It was a startling sight. It stood head to toe at around 5 and a half feet and indeed looked powerful. Not the kind of thing you expect to see in the fens, where the largest bird you are likely to encounter is a Swan or a Heron.

The plan as we had discussed was to try and herd the animal towards the river where we could get a rope around its neck so the farmer could subdue it. We began, walking slowly towards it. I reckon we got to within 100 feet. Then it shot off towards the river. Its speed was unbelievable! Thinking it would stop when it got to the river we followed at a safe distance; however the Ostrich had other ideas and either by design or accident ended up in the river.

The river Nene at March is an old Fenland drain and as such has very steep banks about 10 feet high. Once in the water the Ostrich tried to get out but could not. I thought this would be game over. Get a rope round its neck and drag it out, or whatever but the Ostrich did not wish to give up its freedom that easily. It swam down the river. Swam! I had no idea they could do that. The farmer said that he knew ostrich could swim but had forgotten when we had suggested driving the thing towards the river! The Ostrich now swam up the river like some kind of giant prehistoric Swan, luckily away from town. We followed.

Things were now getting silly. The Ostrich was agitated, hostile and terrified. It was dangerous. It was swimming towards a marina down river, a small holiday park with families and kids present. Also at the marina the banks shallowed off which meant the Ostrich would be able to get out of the river. As I already mentioned the Ostrich was a large adult male and could have badly injured an adult, let alone a child. The end result was at that point sadly quite predictable. I had already anticipated this and asked for the firearms unit to attend. The firearms officers had on occasions dispatched dangerous dogs or other large animals but an animal such as this was a different proposition. Luckily another farmer was present by then (we had attracted a large crowd) and he had a powerful hunting rifle with him. With the owner's permission he shot the Ostrich and killed it. A sad end to what remains one of the most bizarre incidents I ever dealt with.

CHAPTER 5 – SUICIDE

Suicide remains one of the most talked about and controversial subjects today, be it a case of euthanasia, or the results of depression or escaping from crime. There have been many high profile cases of criminals committing suicide with Fred West and Harold Shipman among them. Ian Huntley tried to kill himself soon after he was convicted of killing Holly Wells and Jessica Chapman but was saved (a friend of mine from Ryton had been a medic at the hospital Huntley was taken to and told me several of the staff received threats for saving him).

A lot of people think suicide is a selfish act. I do not know about this at all to be honest. I have seen suicide in many forms over the years and remain undecided. Later towards the end of my career I found myself contemplating whether it was the best choice for me so I feel a small part of the sorrow and helplessness that it must take to allow someone to build the courage to end their life themselves.

However what is a fact that a suicide leaves a body, or remains to be found by someone. Sometimes there is a note, sometimes nothing. Occasionally a suicide is not obvious when the deceased is found, sometimes more so. However you can never know for sure without a thorough investigation. And whatever anyone says being a police officer called to any kind of death is harrowing, be it on a road, in a house or in a public place. A few of my experiences are detailed now.

I had been independent for a few months, and had my driving permit meaning I was driving with blue lights. I was working alone on a day shift in Wisbech, a nearby town when a call came over the radio for a shooting. At the time little was known, apart from a member of the Ambulance service had been called to a male with gunshot wounds. I was the only officer available to attend, and was certainly the closest. I was told to make my way, which I did with firearms supporting from a far corner of the county. I was told strictly to not endanger myself and to certainly not enter the premises.

By the time I arrived at the scene, a remote bungalow in the middle of the Fens I saw a paramedic's vehicle was already at the scene and had been told there was a single occupant of the bungalow with gunshot wounds. However I still did not know exactly what had gone on. We did not know if this was suicide or murder. I conveyed this information over the radio to the control room and a Detective Sergeant was detailed to attend the scene. No other officers were available, apart from the firearm lads who were now heading my way, but under normal driving conditions (no lights/sirens). I deemed it safe to enter to find the paramedic.

We have all seen films. We have all seen people on TV shooting themselves, or being shot in the head with guns and the dramatic, noisy mess it makes. Brains splattered all over the nearest wall, that kind of thing. It was with these mental pictures that I entered the house with a certain sense of trepidation. I loudly identified myself as a police officer upon entry and received a reply from the bedroom I needed to go to. I followed a route through the house, which I would establish as what is known as a common approach path. This was the route all persons entering the premises would follow from that point on, in order to avoid disturbing any potential forensic evidence in the rooms. A CAP involved basically planning a route through a property, avoiding obvious areas where people would tread or touch items, so I stayed to the edge of the room and away from furniture where possible.

Through the entrance hall and living room I came across the master bedroom (it was a two bedroom bungalow). What I then saw certainly gave me pause, and will stay with me until the day I die. A Paramedic was present in the room along with a man, aged in his late thirties who was on the bed, sat up. Beside him was a single barrel shotgun, which looked very old with a rusty barrel and trigger guard and a worn looking wooden stock. It was propped up against the bedside cabinet. The male (who was obviously deceased) was covered in blood, with thick grey tissue and blood having come out of his eyes, ears, nose and mouth soaking his chest and the bed in a grisly tableau. I could not see an entry wound however. Which seemed bizarre since the chap had reportedly been shot. The house was otherwise empty. The room smelled of expended ammunition, mixed with blood. An initial search of the room found no note or any indication that this had been a suicide, and several bottles of methadone (a heroin substitute prescribed by the doctor). Further examination of the bathroom revealed a set of upper dentures, which were covered in blood.

With the above in mind I radioed control to let them know that I felt initially that this was a suspicious death. I could find no entry or exit wound to the front of the victim, my inexperience told me that a shotgun entry wound to the head would be easy to find, so I surmised that any wound must be to the rear of the victim, impossible to inflict yourself. In addition there was the issue of how the dentures had reached the bathroom, the blood on them indicated that they had been removed post mortem.

So as the realisation that I was stood in a potential murder scene dawned on my tiny brain I began talking to the paramedic. Everything was as he found it apart from the fact he had moved the shotgun from the bed.

My first suspicions were quickly allayed. The paramedic had found the shotgun in the deceased's hands when he entered, and pointed out the entry wound to me. The poor man had put the barrel of the shotgun to his eye and pulled the trigger. It was such an old and low powered shotgun that there was no exit wound, but the shot from the cartridge had bounced around inside his skull, destroying any matter in its path, which had done the job he had wanted and killed him instantly. I then found that the 999 call to the ambulance service had been made by the gentleman's daughter, who had found him. She had removed his false teeth on the advice of the ambulance emergency operator before attempting CPR and placed them on the bath later.

These facts took a while to establish and in the meantime a DS had arrived. He stayed as long as to establish the above before leaving me to it, satisfied that there was no foul play. This left me, an inexperienced officer to deal with this terrible and harrowing tragedy alone.

The saddest part of the story was that a succession of relatives began to arrive at the property having heard what was wrong, one of them being the daughter who was in her early 20s. It fell to me to tell each and every one of them that their father, husband, brother, loved one was dead. I had to explain to them all that I had to carry out an investigation and gather evidence for the coroner. I had to sit with the next of kin and complete a sudden death report. This involves asking numerous personal questions about the deceased in order to establish his state of mind, medical conditions and other details which allow the coroner to come to a conclusion as to the cause of death. I learned that the deceased was a heroin addict, but had no convictions for years and was clean. He had been taking methadone and had been off heroin for years. However he had acute depression. He had tried to take his life a week earlier and had been under the local mental health team. It was very sad.

This done the family left the property to be together in their grief, leaving me to continue. I surveyed the rest of the house and to my surprise found upwards of 30 cannabis plants growing in the next bedroom. It was an obvious amateur set-up and for the personal use of the grower (who turned out to be the deceased). The family all knew about it and possibly even shared the crop but I did not think it right to launch a criminal investigation – they were suffering enough and the main perpetrator was now dead. I could not deal with both incidents for obvious reasons and after reporting the matter over the radio two officers appeared to clear the plants. This turned events into a bit of a surreal experience. I was in one bedroom taking photographs of a dead man who had shot himself through the head, not feeling very good about myself; and there were two officers next door cutting up a cannabis farm and to be honest getting a bit giggly on the fumes from the plants. By this time I was glad there was no family around as I half expected to be sent off for some cookies. That's cop humour for you, "if in doubt be flippant" has always been the order of the day among constables. It's a way of coping with it all. If you can make a joke out of it, it can't be that bad can it? Before long the undertaker arrived and took the deceased, and as a favour to me also the bedding as I did not want the family to come back and find blood soaked sheets where their loved one had been. I went back to the police station to complete the paperwork, complete with a variety of Polaroid photographs (we were before the age of the digital camera here). Of course the incident was common knowledge around the area, and as soon as I got in my colleagues all wanted to know about it, and all showed a particular interest in the photographs. I found this macabre fascination in poor taste and also disrespectful. No one had asked me how I was apart from Mick, a close friend on shift and all just seemed to want to look at the pictures to see what a gunshot wound to the head looked like. The few that saw them all made noises of disgust, before saying to the next one "here, have a look at this" I locked myself alone in an office, completed the report and sent it off as quickly as I could.

A couple of months later as the OIC (officer in the case) I was called to give evidence at the inquest. I was treated gently by the coroner, reading my statement to the court with the family looking on. It was a sad story. P had been suffering from

depression and had tried to take his own life two weeks before his eventual suicide by

means of putting a hosepipe on his exhaust and trying to poison himself with the

fumes. He was found and rescued just in time. He had a meeting with the local mental

health team and was willing to be treated, however the day before his suicide his

appointment was cancelled by the team due to a staff shortage of some kind. No one

will ever know if he would be alive today had he made that appointment.

The cause of death was recorded as suicide by means of P shooting himself. I was met

Outside the court by the family and they were extremely gracious and thanked me for

My efforts. It was an emotional and harrowing story and remains vivid in my mind

although it was several years ago. What stays with me is that P's daughter, on finding

her father must have known he was dead, but over the telephone with the ambulance

service she found the courage to try CPR, even taking out her fathers false teeth. Her

loss coupled with this memory makes me feel very ashamed for feeling sad myself, but

at the same time depression is a killer, and this true story highlights this.

Of all the ways in which people take their own life, the most impactful that I

have experienced myself is using a train. This effects not just the person, but the train

driver, signalman, police, and possibly passengers. It is also one of the more "final"

ways of doing it; seldom will someone survive being hit by a train.

This incident happened in a small village called Turves, near to March. The

village is peculiar as it has several level crossings (about three if my memory serves)

within a few hundred yards of each other. The line is the main line linking

Peterborough to March, Cambridge and ultimately London and beyond. There is a lot

of rail traffic and passenger trains will run at speeds of 70mph.

I was called to a report of a pedestrian versus train collision. Officers of the British Transport police would handle the incident, but they were 90 minutes away. It was down to us to attend first and start the investigation, handing over when they arrived. It took me 10 minutes or so to reach the scene and I arrived first. I saw a passenger train stopped up the track, about 500 metres from the crossing involved, and a hundred metres behind it what must have been the pedestrian involved, although it was impossible to tell if it was human. My phrase when updating the control room over the radio was that there was a 'truncated corpse' on the track, and making sure all trains had been stopped reported that I was going to see if the person was still alive.

Donning my yellow reflective jacket (as if that would keep me safe from a train) I walked down the track. It was a gory stroll. At each step I would find a part of the person, some pieces as small as a 10p coin, others recognisable such as hands, bits of gristle and feet, even a toe. Bits littered the track everywhere, punctuated by larger pieces of human remains, such as arms and legs. What was left of the body when I reached it was not recognisable as a human being. There were no limbs and the head was also half-missing, having been sliced in two across the forehead, through the nose and on down in a diagonal line through the torso. I could see some long hair, which was my only clue as to the sex of the poor person. I remember seeing what looked like the other part of the head and returned down the track to find it, containing the person's brain exposed to the elements. It was the goriest thing I have ever seen. The deceased person also had no clothing on, as it had all come apart on impact. All I could say at that point was that it was human, possibly female and of very heavy build (at least 25 stone in weight).

This was the remains of a human being; a living, breathing thinking being and the enormity of the incident hit me. A life was gone. I had to try my best to find out more as much for my own peace of mind as well as the family, if there was one.

By this time another crew arrived, and also had a look. They both came back as green as I did. At that time we had no idea what had happened. The signalman had made the 999 call so the other crew went to see him while I remained at the scene. A paramedic turned up and confirmed that life was extinct while I looked around. Next to the crossing was parked a little car, it had one of those yellow steering locks on it, but the bonnet was warm, indicating it had been parked recently. A check of the index gave me a woman's name and address from a nearby village, not more than a 10-minute drive away. The car had been parked neatly; steering lock applied and it looked all so neat and tidy. Then on the pavement, near to the track at the crossing I found a handbag. It had been left open with a white envelope sticking out, addressed to the police. I opened it and found a suicide note.

It was very sad. The deceased was a lady, who wrote that she had ME. She explained in her letter that she was depressed with no family, the only joy in her life being a menagerie of animals she kept at her home. She explained that she had been an active person, full of life prior to her illness which caused her weight to balloon to the extent she could not look after her animals properly or gain any joy from life. She had decided to end her life, but gave her address and location of a key so her animals could be looked after. She even included information as to where food was and how long it would be before they all needed to be fed again. She ended by apologising to all concerned and hoped we would understand what she had done.

The other officers then came back from speaking to the signalman, and confirmed that he had seen the lady park up, and leave her bag where I found it before going to hide next to the track behind a shed. She then waited until a train came along and star jumped in front of it. Death had obviously been instantaneous. The train was unable to move as it had been damaged and several passengers were very upset, as well as the poor driver.

This is where we had got to when BTP arrived. They took over the management of the scene but we stayed to help, controlling traffic and looking for additional witnesses while we waited for the undertaker.

I thought that the actual walking down the track and discovering the body was bad enough, but it turned out that the BTP officers actually had to pick it all up themselves. This was obviously very important as body parts left behind could later disturbed by animals with the chance they could be found in another location at another date, resulting in a major investigation. The officers donned thick rubber gloves and went about their work, placing all the parts on a rubber sheet. As I said before the lady was very large, and very heavy. The two were carrying her remains on the sheet towards the hearse when suddenly the rubber sheet tore and the body fell to the floor with a sickening and sploshy wet thud. It was horrible and the lads carrying her immediately put the backs of their hands to their mouths, fighting the gag reflex. The undertaker however possessed a sturdier sheet and this was quickly employed and the lady was taken away to the mortuary. An undignified end to what I am sure was meant by the lady to be a dignified and certain end to her life.

The BTP took on the investigation and I heard little further on the matter. The pets were all taken care of and found new homes with loving new owners. It transpired that the dead woman had no relatives alive.

Mental illness is something that is only just being recognised as a real condition that can be as dangerous and as deadly as heart disease, or cancer. The two accounts before relate obviously to someone being so depressed they took their own life, but you can also say that the mental illness came about through something else; drug abuse and ME. The following story happened in the last two years of my career and is about a person suffering from bipolar disorder.

It started as a missing from home report; a missing person if you will. A gentleman had called the police to report that his girlfriend was missing. He had come home for lunch as he always did and found her missing. She was always there. He was concerned as she was Bi-Polar and although not particularly worried she would hurt herself she was in a frail mental state and may be easily led and a target for others. However it was a fairly new relationship, so he was not sure.

I attended the scene to find a very upset man. "L" had not answered any of his phone calls or texts, and there was a quantity of medication (anti-depressants) missing from the house. This was worrying. He had also found a note, which was written with a coloured pencil and was not finished or signed. It only had a couple of lines, "can't take any more, where we walk" was pretty much all it said. There was a child's drawing on the other side. I was very concerned, and radioed my sergeant who attended at once. The first thing I then did was search the house. It sounds like a simple thing but you will be surprised how many missing persons turn up under the bed, or hidden in the loft; particularly in the case of children. It is the first thing the police do and rightly so. As I looked around the house I found several pictures of 'L'. She was a pretty young girl of around 25 and had two children, both young. She looked bright, attractive and full of life in the pictures.

There was a massive, overgrown orchard to the rear of 'L' house a good 5 or 6 acres in size. It was very untidy and full of brambles and high weeds, almost impossible to penetrate. My Sgt. and myself began a search of this area, summoning other officers to assist us. The sergeant's assessment and mine was very grave. Find this woman soon, or we may not find her alive. The boyfriend also went out to search (we could not stop him).

I went into the orchard. It was very hard to walk through and I had been searching for about 20 minutes when from far away I heard the most anguished cries I have ever heard. It was the boyfriend, quickly followed by my Sergeant over the radio asking for urgent assistance. I waded through the orchard to the edge and skirted around it. I found a pathway, which had been marked by a large teddy bear. It was pouring with rain and we were all soaked. I followed the sounds of the shouting and general commotion and saw that 'L' had been found. She had hung herself from an apple tree using a scarf, and by now had been taken down and was lying on her back, with my Sergeant 'B' and colleague 'S' starting attempts at CPR. There was also a member of the public present who was a first aider and he was encouraging and helping the officers. The boyfriend was hysterical, and it fell to me to try and calm him and more importantly get him away from the area to let my colleagues do what they had to do.

It was harrowing. If you have seen someone receiving CPR you will know what an upsetting experience it can be. The heaving and pushing of the chest compressions creates noised from the patients respiratory system which seem like groaning, and the ribs can also crack audibly. I think it was obvious that 'L' was not coming back, as it looked as if she had been there some time but we had to try. Administering CPR is not like you see on the television. It is very hard work. Each compression on the chest requires an effort, and with each one you heard the noise as the air was forced in and out of 'L' chest. Thirty compressions to two breaths. We aimed to keep going until the ambulance arrived with its specialist crew and equipment but this took some minutes; it felt like an hour but was no more than 30 minutes. The paramedics arrived and took over, but quickly gave up. 'L' s airway had closed, we could not get any air into her. She was dead, leaving two children behind. I returned to the house with her boyfriend and completed the paperwork (it all sounds so routine doesn't it)? where I found out more about L. She had had a hard time in the short 25 years she had been alive. She worked at a local homeless shelter and was well loved by staff and residents alike, but in her personal life she had suffered. Her two children were by a man who had abused her over a number of years. He was an alcoholic and it was rumoured that he had even let his grown up son have sex with her. He would beat her and mistreat her on a daily basis. Recently she had found the courage to get out of this abusive marriage. Her new partner, although not violent towards her was an alcoholic also. However he was loving and caring towards her, had stopped drinking and the relationship was moving forward. Both men were much older than L, being middle aged. The relationship with the father of the children had ended recently, and badly. Both her ex-partner and his son hated the new partner, and upon her death various threats were issued. There was a real chance of a further death as a result of this tragedy. I was the officer in the case and with the assistance of a PCSO who was familiar with those involved we drew up a community impact assessment, which is basically a document for the police to risk assess a situation and put plans in place to remedy it. There were rumours going around accusing L's new partner of having murdered her, which were obviously untrue but as you can imagine the community tensions as a result were high. Further problems were avoided but it was a sticky couple of weeks.

After a couple of months the inquest returned a verdict of suicide. I reflected on how a mental illness could have caused a very loving and devoted mother to leave her two children, who ended up living with their father who had at least in part contributed to her condition. Her partner at the time of her death was not involved with the children's lives after that. One small piece of good was that the father of the children stopped drinking and began to address his own life, providing a safe and loving home for his children.

Some suicides are just plain bizarre, or on the face of it seem like suicide but turn out to be something else. Below is possibly the most bizarre death I experienced as a police officer.

I was called to a report of a suicide by hanging at a suburban house on my beat in March. It was reported that a man's father had discovered the body of his son hanging on the landing of his house. It seemed like an obvious case of suicide by hanging at first glance, but on my arrival it became something a lot more serious, before becoming something that none of us had experienced before.

I arrived at the scene and on entering the house found an elderly gentleman and the deceased. The deceased was not hanging as outlined to me over the radio; he was lying on the stairs. His head was about eighteen inches from the top of the stairs and he was lying on his back with his feet near to the bottom. I could clearly see a blue nylon rope tied to the banister post at the top of the stairs, which was tight with the weight of the deceased pulling on it. The rope was also clearly around the neck of the deceased but was not tight, rather a crude fixed loop had been tied and placed around the neck, but this did not act as a noose leaving the front of the throat cut off but the back of the neck untouched. I also should say that the deceased was naked, and there were signs that the deceased had ejaculated. Initially this gave no cause for concern as the man was firstly in his own home and could go around as naked as a baby if he so wished, and secondly when a male person dies in this manner I had heard that it is quite common for him to ejaculate.

At this point no paramedic or member of the ambulance service had arrived so death had not been recognised, other than by the deceased persons father who told me that he had not checked, only saying that to him it was clear he was dead. The father seemed very calm, but this can be normal in shocking cases such as this so my suspicions were not piqued at that point.

I climbed the stairs in order to check the deceased person's pulse (taking great care not to tread on him) and on feeling around his neck with a gloved hand found none. It was quite obvious that he was dead, and had been for some hours as the blood in his body had pooled to the lower part of his legs and back. This happens post mortem as the heart stops pumping the blood succumbs to gravity and 'pools' at the lowest parts and is clearly visible through the skin as redness.

As I checked the pulse however I saw a hammer at the top of the stairs where the deceased's head lay. On closer examination I could see hair on it, the same colour as the deceased's. Again, on examination of the deceased I could see that there was an obvious injury to his head, at the back around three inches from his ear.

At this point I had a dead body, naked, hanging down the stairs with a hammer with hair on it and a matching wound to the deceased persons head. The deceased's father told me that his brother had also committed suicide and he had lost other family members who had also taken their own life.

What would you think of this? CID was quickly called and a detective sergeant arrived shortly afterwards. The scene was preserved while crime scene investigators moved in.

So, for the amateur sleuths among you all, how did this man die? Was he murdered or did he actually take his own life?

Well the answer is that he did take his own life, but did not intend to. Erotic asphyxiation, where you cut off your oxygen supply when at the point of orgasm was not well known when this incident happened; the well-publicised death of the rock star Michael Hutchence being the only example I knew of. But this death was caused by the same thing.

The deceased had tied the rope to the banister post while his father slept and applied the rope to his neck. This did not provide the required level of force to cause the starvation of oxygen necessary to achieve the desired results so he tightened the noose by sticking the handle of the hammer into the loop and twisting it (making a makeshift garrotte) while he masturbated.

Somehow, either in the act or orgasm or by twisting too hard the deceased let go of the hammer causing it to spin, this created enough force for the hammer to hit his head and knock him out cold. The weight of his body from here was enough that while he was unconscious he slowly asphyxiated himself.

CHAPTER 6 – MENTAL HEALTH.

Mental health is still, even now seen as a stigma by some, made up by others and little known by the majority. As a police officer I came across many incidents that had been caused by a person's mental health, and later on came to see that your mental health is like any other important organ in your body. If something is wrong it is just as serious than a problem with your brain, heart, kidneys or any other important part of your anatomy you should care to name. In particular, mental health issues are a killer of people and are not to be ignored or underestimated. Here is why.

I will start with something that is on the lighter side of life. Regular callers into the police force. You will have read stories from blogs, books and social media telling stories about people who have called 999 for a policeman to come and change a light bulb, or kids calling 999 in a public phone kiosk and any number of other silly reasons. These are all very funny even though they are a drain on valuable resources, but another very large thing that takes up time in a police control room and for officers on the ground is the regular caller. Regular callers are just as they sound; it is a person who will call the police literally hundreds or thousands of times a year, usually more than ten times a day. That's more than 3600 calls a year! These people are not criminals, and many have a mental health issue of some kind. Here are two examples.

One lady I will always remember is a middle-aged woman living near to Saint Ives. She was an intelligent and forthright person and lived alone. However she had a problem with one of her neighbours which had been mediated by a local constable, who I will refer to as M. M had dealt with this community issue, but not to R's satisfaction so she began to call the police on a regular basis to complain and vent her spleen on whoever was on the other end of her telephone at that particular time (i.e. me or another of my colleagues).

I say a regular basis, but she would not ring every day. But on the days she did ring it was always on the 999 system, and when she got a head of steam up she would call 50 or so times in the space of an hour. These calls were always made in a high pitched screeching noise and were filled with foul language and allegations made against constable M. She alleged an affair had taken place between them, and as a married man M should be sacked, imprisoned, drawn, quartered and burned at the stake. When you answered a 999 call you would always firstly ask the operator for the number of the caller before addressing the person with "police emergency how can I help?" Most of the time the operator would not be able to get the number across to me due to the shouting at the other end and would have to mute her. We would try talking to her, reassuring her, referring her to the local sergeant or inspector or simply hanging up after telling her to stop misusing the 999 system but nothing worked. She would tie up the 999 lines for a whole afternoon with this. She was well known and seen as a mad old woman by all staff but it was serious when real emergencies could not get through because an operator was tied up with her. B was even arrested on a couple of occasions and even taken to court for doing this. She would go quiet for a week or so and then start up again. Eventually she was sectioned under the mental health act and received the help she so desperately needed.

W was a man living in Peterborough. He was a small, thin man who had fallen upon hard times. I believe he was seriously ill with a mental health illness but to this day do not know what became of him. His story goes like this.

I took my first call from W one night shift at around midnight. He was not known to any of us as a regular caller at this time. He called from his flat in Peterborough. He told me that he was feeling very depressed and wanted to self-harm. He also had a knife in his hand. I took him at face value and immediately raised an 'A' grade incident, sending it over to dispatch for an officer to attend immediately. I chatted to W for a long time (over 30 minutes), him telling me about how his son had been taken from him and lived with his ex-wife and how his life had fallen apart. On several occasions he told me he was cutting himself and was going to die. To be on the other end of the phone to this is a sobering experience and I believed every word he said. I thought he was cutting and stabbing himself as he talked to me. Officers arrived at his flat and could not get in. I waited on the phone trying to persuade W to open to door but he refused, telling me he wanted to die.

Officers forced entry to find W perfectly OK, with a beer I his hand but certainly no knife. A lot of police time had been wasted, including armed response units and a dog handler. Additionally an ambulance had been called to the scene as well.

This was the first call of thousands from W. He managed to fool several operators into long calls where he received a lot of attention both from them and also police officers on the ground. If he received no reaction he would continue to call again and again, dozens of times a night. He never once harmed himself during this time. Once we got wise to this he began embellishing, telling us he had a knife and was going to harm others. This could not be ignored and he received still more attention. After a while he was evicted from his flat and moved into a YMCA. He had no phone now, so used a phone box outside the place to call 999. Sometimes he would not speak just to see the police attending. Eventually he was arrested for wasting police time and given a caution. This did not stop him, and after two more arrests he was imprisoned. He would go quiet for a month or so after his release but would always start up again. He was still doing it when I joined the force as a police officer five years later.

M eventually stopped being a regular caller. I heard on the rumour mill that her accusations towards B were actually genuine but I do not know if this is true at all. What I do know is that M was ill and although she caused no harm to others, the hours lost to her detracted from officers being in other areas.

W it turns out, was a bad man. It transpired that he lost his wife through cruelty to her and his son was taken by social services as he neglected him. Left alone without an audience his guilt fed his depression and he descended into frenzy, wanting attention from any source available. He also made calls to the ambulance service of the same nature, but the police bore the brunt of his efforts. What was clear though was that D had a mental health condition that had caused or at least contributed to all of his behaviour, well before he began calling 999. These calls were a nuisance a massive drain on resources, but as with M, W' calls were possibly the only human contact, and perhaps comfort in their very lonely and solitary lives.

Sometimes people with mental health problems can be extremely violent, or do reckless things that can endanger them and others around them. There is a piece of legislation called section 136 of the mental health act that gives a police officer power to detain a person in a public place if he or she feels that person is at imminent risk of serious harm, or to those around them. I used this legislation to detain many people over my career and to be honest when I look back it turns my stomach to remember how some of the mentally ill were treated.

One character (and he was in every sense of the word) was a man I will call J. He was a paranoid schizophrenic and lived in March and was a fantastic funny character when in a good mood, but an evil little shit otherwise. He lived alone and to be fair did not take good care of himself, habitually smoking a large amount of cannabis every day and drinking to excess. It was not a recipe for any person to lead a healthy lifestyle, but with his condition for J it was a path to disaster. J had a love hate relationship with his mother, in that she loved him but he seemed to hate her, going by the way he treated her. This however did not stop him from going to her house and demanding money, food or whatever else he wanted at that particular time. It sounds like something that happens with many parents and is relatively normal, but J would be particularly aggressive about this and on a bad day would smash windows, and threaten to harm his mother on more than one occasion by chasing her with a knife. It was on one such occasion that he had smashed a window that I found him in a very agitated state on the road outside her house and had no option but to detain him under sect 136. I put him in my van (he was not aggressive to me and never was on the many occasions I came into contact with him) and radioed that I had detained him and was heading to the custody suite at Wisbech Police Station, a 30 minute drive.

One of my biggest issues with dealing with patients detained under Section 136 of the Mental Health Act was at that time; the custody suite was where you took them. The logic was that the main priority was to get the person to a place of safety, where a doctor can be called to assess them. This was a time consuming process and the doctor often took many hours to arrive, which obviously did not do any good for the detainee who had normally committed no crime. Violence or erratic behaviour from mental health detainees was common, and in some cases almost understandable.

On my arrival at Wisbech I was informed that a new mental health suite for Sect 136 detainees had been set up at Kings Lynn Hospital, a further 30-minute drive away. It meant that J would be in the back of my van for an hour in total, but at least he would now be going straight to a place where he would be seen by a Mental health Professional quickly. We arrived at Kings Lynn and I escorted J to what turned out to be a small waiting room. J was agitated and was also in handcuffs as I was alone and was responsible for his safety as well as my own. He had a history of absconding and handcuffs were the only way I could detain him safely. I had been assured that someone would meet us upon our arrival but this did not materialise. I spent an hour on the phone trying to sort things out but no one appeared. I was then told I needed to take J to Peterborough Hospital instead, which was another hours drive away. As I told J this I could see that he was upset. I would not want another hour in the back of a van either. By this time he had been in my custody for over two hours, and had at least another hour to go. I might add that he had been in handcuffs throughout this time also.

I took J to Peterborough where thankfully we were able to get him seen very quickly. The point of telling this story is to highlight the inadequacy of how police have to deal with mental health patients, and this person who had not committed a serious crime was left waiting for over three hours before he got to a place of safety.

Another quick tale about J, with whom I came into contact on a semi regular basis. J was prone to doing stupid things when ill. He was a habitual cannabis user and a drinker, which played havoc with his moods and fed his paranoia. Sometimes, when off his medication he would lose it and go and do something daft. This was one such occasion; it nearly cost him his life.

It was a summer's day in March. Very pleasant. I had taken myself out on foot patrol in the town centre, which I did every day whenever I had the time. I was some 100 metres from the Town Bridge; which is the bridge in the centre of town over the old course of the river Nene. The Nene is a small river, and through town is only four feet or so deep. The riverbed under the bridge was solid concrete. I had seen and spoken to J earlier in my patrol and he seemed OK, but when I was called over the radio to the a report of a person having jumped off the town bridge into the river I knew straight away it would be J. It only took me seconds to get to the bridge where I saw J scrambling back up the bank towards a bus shelter, known locally as the "old man shelter". As J was walking I made an assumption that he was OK. However as I approached him I could see things were very different. On speaking to witnesses J had dived off the side of the bridge, entering the river head first. On looking at J I could see blood running down his face from obvious wounds to his skull. In fact the blood was running all around his head. An ambulance was called and I had a major task keeping J still and calm while we waited. Thankfully it was only five minutes before the ambulance arrived. I had examined J's wounds closely. Not only was his scalp cut but it was clear his skull was badly fractured, I could see bits of bone sticking up everywhere and frankly was amazed he could still walk and talk. When the paramedic looked with a torch he showed me exactly the extent of his injuries and the fact that in one place J's brain was visible and open to the elements. The injury reminded me of a boiled egg that you have hit on the top with a spoon. J however was not going along with the programme and refused to go to hospital. This is in the days before the mental capacity act where you could make a decision on a person's behalf in their best interests if you judged they lacked the mental capacity to make it for themselves. All at this point that we could rely on was persuasion, for me in the form of telling J frankly that he had a fractured skull and I could see his brain; if he did not go to hospital he would die. J went.

I was confident that J would now be looked after by the right people, and finally sectioned under the mental health act and given the right treatment. I was wrong. The next day amazingly I saw J walking around in town with a massive bandage around his head. He told me that his fractures had been put together a bit like a jigsaw so he discharged himself. I was amazed this had been allowed to happen, but not surprised. It turns out J was not mentally ill enough! I mused, as how poorly one would need to be to actually receive the help one needed. I know of course that J would have resisted being detained but surely he should have been sectioned as a result of his actions? No was the sad answer.

In the nearly ten years since this incident occurred I am happy to say that the awareness and treatment of mental health issues has improved dramatically. Police now have access to special suites so that persons detained under the Mental Health Act can receive the professional help they require immediately. I was to learn myself from my own experience that the treatment given to mental health patients by the NHS today is now second to none.

CHAPTER 7 - ROAD TRAFFIC COLLISIONS

Road Accidents are a specialist incident and the most serious are investigated by highly qualified collision investigators and traffic officers. They do a fantastic job at the scenes of fatal or serious injury accidents and the astounding evidence they can produce is based on science as well as investigative skill. Their expertise is unrivalled; they can measure the smallest mark on the road (even the scrape left by a pedestrians footwear when struck by a car) and deduce so many things about the vehicles speed and position on the road. However these officers are seldom the first officers to arrive at the scene of a serious accident, as they are a force wide resource often far away from the scene. It is the local Bobbies covering response whom are often the first to arrive and manage the first minutes of a scene. Successful prosecutions and investigations are often related directly to the actions of the first officer to arrive. A serious Road Traffic Collision is first and foremost a potential crime scene, in extremes even a murder. For a person with a semi decent knowledge of the law, one of the most fool proof ways to murder someone is with a motor vehicle. It is very hard to prove a murder in these scenarios and the more likely charge would be causing death by dangerous driving, which carries a far shorter sentence. Often collision scenes are ruined evidentially by the milling around of the emergency services as they battle to save lives, which is unavoidable.

The accounts I am going to give here are not murders. But for me personally they were the root cause of a severe mental illness and ultimate dismissal from the police service in 2013. Little did I know at the time, but the events surrounding the two incidents below were to be played back and forth in my mind a hundred times a day for over six years.

Halloween 2007. I was single crewed on a late shift in March. It was roughly 1730 in the early evening and I was on patrol in a panda car. A report of an RTC came in over the radio, car versus a horse on Leverington Common; a remote Fenland road near to Wisbech. I responded and made my way on blues and twos. As I travelled more information came in via the ambulance service who had received further 999 calls. It was not just a horse and a car. There were pedestrians involved, including children. The information filtered through as I drove and I hastened in the wintery conditions to the scene. It took me about ten minutes, and I was the second police officer to arrive.

The events that followed my arrival and those I found preceded it will stay with me forever more.

As I have already stated the scene was a dark country road with no street lighting. It was pitch back and cold, very remote.

I was the second police officer to arrive at the scene. The first was a colleague, K who had joined about six months after me and arrived at the scene 30 seconds or so before me. I did not see much of K after our initial contact on arrival. After a while I learned that she had resumed from the scene as it caused such a profound reaction in her. Anyway, as I said I did not see her much, only to wave as I saw her the other side of an Ambulance that had arrived before us.

From then on and for the next three hours I was busy trying to stop myself from blubbing and to do my job professionally and with compassion. As I said, I saw an ambulance and the paramedic had just climbed down. There was a little girl lying on the road, she was four or so years old and had long golden hair. She was uncannily like my own youngest daughter. Just lovely. However the paramedic was looking her over with a very pained expression and as I went to assist him it was clear that she was not breathing nor had any heartbeat. As I knelt next to her the paramedic began to start compressions and giving the little girl breaths in order to try and revive her. It was not looking very hopeful and after a second kneeling there holding her hand I had to carry on with my assessment of the scene and casualties. Such a pretty little girl. I had tears in my eyes from that moment. I have mentioned before that to witness CPR in the real world is in itself an upsetting experience but on a child? Well I will leave it to your imagination to decide how you would feel. I wanted nothing more than to stay with this little girl but there was important work to do.

My first priority was to preserve life, and after that establish a scene in order to preserve evidence. This was particularly tough with emergency services still arriving. I had been with the child for a few seconds, or maybe minutes or hours; who knows? But I had a job to do. My radio was non-stop chatter. I clearly radioed an update back advising no other officers were to enter the scene in order to preserve evidence and there was one likely to prove fatal casualty and possibly others as yet unidentified. More Ambulances were arriving and I did not want to fill the area with too many other vehicles and people. Medical aid at that time was my priority in that moment. Other mobiles did arrive and in the background put in place road closures or diversions. I was unaware of them completely until officers from the traffic department turned up when I would guess I had been there for 30 minutes or so. This all happened over the space of a few minutes I guess, but I don't really know. However going back to the beginning, I left the little girl in the hands of the medical staff and carried on.

Just feet away on the road lay a woman. She was I would guess in her thirties and was lying on her back. She was fully conscious and again I knelt beside her to have a short conversation and to check on her condition. Her legs were broken which you did not need to be a doctor to diagnose looking at them but as yet no help was forthcoming. The Paramedics were at that time still arriving and were frantically working on the little girl who was by now in an ambulance. I could see the bones sticking out at odd angles from her jeans. She was in pain but not bleeding and at that time was certainly not in immediate danger of death from her injuries and was alert and talking to me. During our conversation I learned that there had been four pedestrians, the lady I was talking to was leading her daughter who was sat astride a pony. Her friend was pushing her own daughter in a buggy. She said a car had come up behind them and hit them. They had only just left the house and were off trick or treating. She was frantic about her daughter (whom I found apart from cuts and a few bruises was OK; the height of being up on the horse having protected her from harm). The other mother however was nowhere to be seen at this time. She asked about the other child and mother but at that time I stayed quiet.

By now it was clear that this was going to be a serious incident involving several casualties. I radioed control again letting them know what I had found out at that point and also that I recommended that this become a critical incident. This meant that a high-ranking officer would manage the incident and the impact on the wider community be assessed; with things like media and community impact planned and controlled from the outset.

There had been no sign of the horse, which was a worry as such a large animal was likely to do serious injury if it bolted through the scene, or onto the road at another place. To be honest I did not think about it much as there were other more pressing things at hand.

The vehicle, which had struck the group from behind, was partially in the shallow dyke to the near side (left) of the road; it was on its side along the dyke with one side pressed down on the inner wall of it. In the absence of the missing lady I guess I knew straight away where she would be found.

A quick glimpse was all it took. The mother of the little girl was underneath the vehicle. I could not be sure but it seemed obvious she was dead from the look of her. I quickly shouted that I had found another casualty and left the rest to paramedics and fire service. A short time later her death was confirmed.

What next? I had established a scene, the road was closed and by now all the casualties were being assessed and treated. The horse had also been located, also dead, in the adjacent field.

What was next was the driver of the vehicle. Collision investigators were still a long way off and I had to establish who the driver was, find any witnesses and try and find out what the hell had happened here.

There was a group of three people standing near the car, two young men and an older woman. One of the young men (from memory he was 18 or so) identified himself to me as the driver. I quickly took him and his mother and friend away from the area. The reason I did this was that the father of the dead mother and child had appeared, they lived less than 50 yards from the scene and he had heard the commotion and become worried. Other officers helped with him and he did not yet know that he had lost his daughter and grandchild. Selfishly I did not want him to find out and then make a connection with the lad standing next to the car responsible, as understandably he would be angry, upset and deeply aggrieved and I did not wish for these unpredictable emotions to spill over into an attempt at retribution.

I took the driver away, and did a breath test on him, which was completely clear. Following this I had to establish the identities of all involved and then interview the driver, under caution. This was not a full interview but his first account of the accident; he would be interviewed in fine detail (probably videoed as well) at a later date. I then took accounts from the passengers in the vehicle. I had to keep from him the information that he would almost certainly be arrested when traffic officers arrived.

As you can imagine the driver was extremely shaken. He had not had his licence long and told me that he was just driving along; not speeding and the people and horse just appeared in front of him. He said he could not do anything about it. At the time the road was pitch dark. There were no street lights and although one of the mothers was wearing a reflective jacket she was in front of the horse so was obscured and probably not visible to the driver. It fell to me to tell the driver that people had died. He was quite obviously shocked and upset by this. I also warned him that there of course would be a full investigation and that he would be questioned at a later time. I asked him to not leave the area and waited for the traffic lads to arrive. He was later arrested on suspicion of dangerous driving at the scene. This in itself is no cause for alarm, but the police need to lead a prompt and effective investigation and the immediate arrest was necessary for this.

I think I had been at the scene around two hours as these events unfolded. The Road Policing Unit arrived and the specialists took over. I was released from the scene and I was glad to be. It had been a harrowing couple of hours and I was mentally and physically exhausted. The sorrow and compassion I felt for the families of those who were dead or injured filled me and all I really wanted to do was see my own children; both little girls and hold and cuddle them. The RPU would now survey the scene and gather evidence, which would take several hours. The car would be recovered and examined and the undertakers would collect the deceased mother. Every mark on the road would be analysed, photographed and copied and every measurement imaginable would be taken. The little girl I spoke of at the beginning had been rushed to hospital but having been one of the first to her I knew all was likely to be lost.

I got back to my vehicle and followed the diversion around the scene to go to Wisbech Police Station. I only got as far as the back yard. I parked up and got out of the car. I wanted to go to the toilet, have a coffee and a fag and try and settle my mind down a bit. All the other officers that had been to the scene were upstairs in the nick having a debrief and basically being looked after. That was upsetting; I was one of the first member of the emergency services to arrive, did most of the initial work at the scene and was the last divisional officer to leave, but I had seemingly been forgotten or ignored. I went into the station and found the briefing door closed, so I went for a comfort break and went out to the back yard again and had a fag. Whilst doing this my radio went off… it was the divisional inspector. "Have you resumed from the RTC?" He asked, "If so I need you to go back to March to attend a Burglary". That was that. Off I went. I went off to the burglary and was late off finishing up with statements for the RTC.

The following day I got to work and had received an email from my Sergeant who had been stuck in custody the previous night and had not been involved. He apologised for my being let down and not supported but other than that nothing happened. I did not want to say anything about it as I did not want to make a fuss and seem like I wanted attention. I should have. I should have asked for help. If I knew than what I know now I would have done. Funnily enough the local superintendent sent round an email congratulating all the officers involved for a professional job. I was left out. I got a copy of it when a colleague emailed her explaining I had been missed off. Funny Old World! I did not want any praise or credit especially but it would have been nice if I had not been forgotten.

This collision and the tragedy behind it was very high profile in the community and made the national press six months later, when the CPS decided that no charges would be brought against the driver. The victims, a 25 year old mother and her 4 year old child were pictured just before they went out on their walk together. What should have been a fun evening trick or treating for them all turned to tragedy in a second. Two lives wiped out, one a child. The inquest returned a verdict of accidental death.

The Fenland area if you do not know it is renowned for being flat. In its history it was mostly flooded until it was drained by the Dutch who built a system of drains and windmills to drain the land, leaving wide swathes of fertile land now famous for crops. What is left know are dozens of dykes and drains that criss-cross the flat bleak landscape. Any of these drains are long, wide, deep and straight and have roads built along the sides of their steep banks. These roads are notorious accident black spots and over the years dozens of people have died in the drains through cars entering the water. I will talk about one such accident now.

21st February 2008. Just under four months since the tragic events of Leverington Common the previous Halloween and I was again on a late shift in March.

A general call went out for officers to attend an RTC on the 16-Foot bank, near a place known as Bedlam Bridge. A car had entered the water and occupants were said to be trapped inside.

I immediately made my way, to this remote location on icy roads, which lay about 8 miles from March. I often patrolled the 16-foot bank and knew the river had been iced over and would be very cold. I had been to accidents here before, only recently attending a vehicle in the water where a passer-by had bravely rescued a mother and her two children after their car went in at the same bridge. It was a bit nonsensical as the road itself was dead straight, but cars kept going in the river through stupid overtaking and too much speed. A local campaign had been going some time to improve safety on this stretch.

On route myself and all other officers attending had received orders that we were not to enter the water under any circumstances.

I was the first officer to arrive at the scene. I found a car submerged in the water three quarters of the way across the bank from the road, only the tailgate was visible. Two passers-by had witnessed the car going in and had jumped into the water, managing to rescue the driver who was a lady. I found out quickly that there was a child trapped in the vehicle, which had been submerged for around ten minutes.

At this point I will outline the cold water training police officers get. Nothing. Only a few words in a classroom amounting to "don't go in" were uttered. I was a bit luckier as I had an input from a private company contracted to carry out all cold water rescue on behalf of the police which amounted to the same. Their exact words were "If the person is under for over ten minutes it's not a rescue, it's a recovery".

Bearing in mind what I faced here. Two members of the public had already risked themselves by entering the water and had rescued the mother. When a police officer arrived at the scene I am sure they expected me to rescue the child with all the training and kit I carry in my car. They are not to know my training was meagre, and my kit consisted of only a throw rope.

With the orders to not go in ringing in my ears and the picture I saw in front of me I decided that I would indeed enter the water and attempt a rescue. I knew the water would be freezing and I was not a strong swimmer but I could not stand by at the side of a river while a mother watches her child drowning.

I began to prepare to enter the water. Off came my body armour, belt kit on which my cuffs and baton were attached and I emptied my pockets. As I did this another police officer arrived. "N" was a mate who had left the firearms team because he wanted to work for a living; he is a good lad and well respected. We conferred for a second and he told me he could swim well, and was better served to go in. We had both been told to not go in but here we were arguing which one of us would disobey orders. We decided that "N" would go in. I suggested we drove to the other bank using a farm track as that was closer to the car and we used up a minute doing this, but we both felt that this would reduce the risks to N. That done N stripped as I had and I tied a rope around his waist, holding the other end as N went in holding nothing but a life hammer to try and smash the rear windows. I held onto the rope and stood at the water's edge, just managing to get my feet wet. N got out to the car, but could not get any of the doors open, nor smash the windows. As he were out there other officers arrived and made their way to the bank. N was inches from where the child was but could not get to her. He did not give up and kept trying.

We all knew a nine-year-old little girl was in the back of the car and we were desperate. I even suggested we tie a rope to the car and between us we tried to physically pull the car to the side but it was too heavy.

Other emergency services arrived. An ambulance pulled up and immediately set up a station on the far bank to treat Charlotte when she was taken from the vehicle. The force helicopter also arrived, landing only 20 metres from us. The crew shouted to bring the child straight to them if we got her out and they would fly her over the river to the waiting ambulance to save time. It really was a fantastic effort from everyone. The bank was loud with discussion between us as to what to do next, what can we try to get Charlotte from the water. We had all heard tales of people surviving after several minutes underwater.. we had hope.

The Fire brigade arrived also on the far bank along with my Sergeant "C" (from the Ostrich saga).. "C" had previously given the order for us to stay out of the water, but now stripped off and dove straight in from the far bank, swimming out to "N". I was relieved when Fire arrived… I thought that they would be carrying the equipment to go in the water themselves and quickly rescue Charlotte and give her a fighting chance. I was wrong. The Fireman too had been ordered to not enter the water and they did what they were told. I make no judgements, although I was angry at the time and bore a grudge for many years afterwards. I realise now that they were acting on orders and contrary to what we had done had obeyed them. At the end of the day they have a responsibility to make sure they do not put themselves and put others in danger in order to rescue them.

That in mind we knew that the Fire Engine (or appliance as they called it) had a winch on it. I suggested that they winch the car to their side so that Charlotte could be removed from the car. By this time it had been at least 25 or 30 minutes since the car entered the water. C swam back to the far bank and got a rope. He swam back to the car and threw the rope back so that the winch could be attached and pulled it back to him where he attached it to the car. N had been in the water for at least twenty Minutes and C 15. The car was towed to the far bank and the waiting fireman got Charlotte out of the car. It's an image that sticks in my head with all the rest. She was swiftly put into the waiting station and worked upon by the Ambulance staff. The news we got in the first minutes was that the Ambulance staff had begun working and were hopeful. I believe they had got a pulse. Charlotte was taken to hospital immediately but as the time went on we found that she had indeed passed away soon after arriving at Hospital.

N and C were also taken to hospital with hypothermia. Both recovered OK but it was obviously a worrying time for them both as well as their colleagues and families. This was now a fatal RTC and the RPU (Road Policing Unit) would attend. I again remained at the scene establishing a road closure on Bedlam Bridge, looking down through the darkness at the scene with tears in my eyes before again being one of the last officers to leave. I looked and felt awful, and was distraught. After the incident at Halloween I was not ready for this, another child death. Pasty had attended the scene also and reported to control that I was visibly shaken. I resented this a little, as I did not want to be singled out, however he was acting out of compassion and I value his care and friendship at that time immensely.

When I got back to the station I remember the Chief Inspector, who had stayed on to see her staff safely back. She was lovely, gave me a cuddle in fact, which is something you do not expect from a senior officer.

The shift did not end there. Soon afterwards I was called to another accident on the A142 near Chatteris. An elderly male had crashed his car into a fence, narrowly missing a building and was seriously injured. I went to the scene and saw the man, but thankfully was not involved too much. I went and put a road closure on before being relieved on the orders of the chief inspector (I had had enough). The poor man also passed away in hospital meaning I had been to two fatal accidents in that shift (Five in four months since October).

I completed my paperwork as to what happened during the shift and went off duty. I got home and got straight into bed with my youngest daughter who was at that time 5, complete with my boots on. She gave daddy a big cuddle and a kiss, which was all the comfort I wanted. I was not to know the full impact of what I had seen and done for a long time afterwards.

Charlotte's death was not in vain. Since the accident a number of safety measures have been introduced on the stretch of road involved. C and N were given high commendations by the Royal Humane society for their bravery that day. Two other officers and myself were also awarded Royal Humane Society awards for our actions. We were presented with them at a ceremony a year or so after the event. I am proud of the award in a way, but I do not display it as it does seem very empty compared with our failure to rescue Charlotte in time. I will remember that little girl always.

CHAPTER 8 – DOMESTIC VIOLENCE

A lot of what I hear from friends and family outside the Police is how they could not do the job of a Police Officer as they would not be able to keep their temper in check, particularly in cases of Domestic Violence. It is true that men who attack women are the scum of the earth and that a large percentage of violent crime is related to violence inside the home. I have seen all types of Domestic violence and the effect it has on the victim, offender and families and have spent countless hours in the company of perpetrators, victims, and witnesses.

The way in which the Police deal with domestic violence has changed radically over the last decade which is all for the better. For example the very definition of domestic violence is now clear and encompasses all types of abuse on top of the obvious physical violence that often hits the headlines. The way in which police officers at the scene of Domestic violence is now much changed. In the bad old days if we got to a domestic, and the victim refused to divulge what went on or refused to make a criminal complaint we would leave, doing nothing to safeguard the victim. A crime for Domestic would be raised but there would be no other action. Nowadays every report of Domestic violence is investigated and the risk to all parties will be assessed using the DASH matrix. This is a booklet containing set questions, the answer for each attracting a score. At the end of the booklet the scores are added and the total gives you a risk level, low, medium or High. High-risk victims will be followed up discussed at a MARAC meeting where additional support and investigation will be offered, with concerted efforts made to safeguard their safety. Children involved in domestic violence as victims or witnesses are also safeguarded. I believe firmly that police deal with domestic violence in a positive and effective way and the lives of many victims are now saved.

I will relate a few of my experiences in regard to domestic violence here.

Dealing with Domestics, as a first responder was one of the more common incidents I attended during my service. It was never pleasant and often disturbing and harrowing.

On one particular shift I was working overtime to support a shift who were short on staff. I had been called in on my rest day and was on "double bubble", and was happy to be earning a few extra quid. I was working a night shift, 2200 until 0600.

On arrival I was quickly accosted by the duty sergeant and given a prisoner to deal with. The prisoner concerned was in custody on suspicion of a serious assault on his girlfriend who was at that time in hospital being treated. He was drunk so would not be fit to be interviewed for some hours.

Basically at this point that was the sum total of the information I had, but the arresting officer was in the process of completing a handover package, which would contain more information for me which would enable me to get an interview in to get the prisoner through custody.

More often than not, domestic violence cases are complicated. Sometimes the victim will refuse to co-operate with the police, either through fear of the defendant or misguided loyalty. In addition to that often the victim is in a moral quandary as they are in love with the perpetrator and do not want to get them in trouble Also there are seldom any witnesses in cases of domestic assault as nine times out of ten it happens behind closed doors. Often witness evidence is hearsay or circumstantial, in that the victim has confided in friends or family that abuse has happened but the friend or family member has actually not seen any abuse taking place. Especially problematic is proving historical abuse where there is no record of physical evidence to present. Having been provided with the handover package and viewing the contents it was obvious that I had more work to do. The victim was in hospital in Huntingdon and at that point had not been spoken to. The offence had happened in Wimblington, a village near March and the prisoner was in the cells at Wisbech. It was a thirty five-mile drive from the victim to the offender and the offence location was in the middle somewhere. There were statements from a couple who were witnesses and from those I was able to glean some of the nights events up until that point. The victim "H" and her boyfriend "A" were on a double date with the two witnesses. They had a meal at the witnesses' home and went out for a few drinks at the local pub before going back to the friends for more drinks. It was at that point the assault happened. All parties were drunk and there had been some good-natured flirting going on between H and one of the witnesses. According to the witness it was all banter and in good humour; no one took it seriously. All appeared to be well. "A" and "H" went out into the back garden for a cigarette while the witnesses stated inside. After a few minutes both witnesses heard screaming and shouting and upon going outside found "H" on the ground curled up in a ball with "A" standing over her. "A" stormed out and an ambulance was called with police following soon after. It was then said that "A" had lashed out at "H" knocking her to the floor and then kicking her repeatedly while she was defenceless.

It is worth mentioning that "H" was a woman in her late thirties and was slim in build with no criminal convictions and a sound character. "A" was a male in his early forties, fit and well built. He was in fact a former paratrooper.

I made a phone call to the hospital to try and gain an update into the victims condition and was told she had severe bruising all over her body, but had suspected internal injuries. I arranged for local officers to attend the Hospital and try and get an update and if possible speak to the victim and get a first account.

What was clear early on was that this was a sickening assault on a woman by a strong powerful man. I still had no clue as to what caused it, and no eyewitness to the assault itself.

After a further hour or so, during which I prepared myself for an interview with the suspect I got the first account from the victim. She was sedated and had not given a full account, but she had confirmed she had been assaulted by "A" and had been kicked and stamped on whilst on the ground. This posed a change in severity for me. "A" had been arrested under suspicion of assault occasioning Actual Bodily harm; a serious enough offence in itself but I felt that the stamping and repeated kicking demonstrated intent to cause injury amounting to Grievous bodily Harm, and this was the charge I would ultimately go for. In my opinion the defendant would or should have known that stamping repeatedly on the victim whilst on the ground was likely to cause serious injury. When dealing with any case a police officer will always remain impartial as a person is innocent until proven guilty. But occasionally you do struggle to do this. My blood was boiling. I wanted to nail him to the wall.

With that in mind I contacted the Detective Sergeant on duty, as the severity of this assault demanded that a more qualified investigator (A Detective Constable or Domestic Violence specialist) took over. However this was not possible. It was now the middle of the night and there was only one DC on in the division overnight, who was responsible for all serious crime that went on. It was either leave the prisoner until the morning, bail him without interview or I deal with him. There was no chance option two was viable as the victim needed to be safeguarded and the custody sergeant did not want the prisoner in all night either. I dealt with him. It was unusual for a PC to deal with a GBH but this was borderline, and I was also a reasonably competent interviewer and experienced PC.

When dealing with any prisoner in custody as is right and proper they have access to legal advice and representation during the time they are in police custody free of charge. Therefore the first task was to await the arrival of the solicitor and brief them; something called disclosure. Disclosure was obviously the first time that the police would discuss the case with the defendant through their legal representative who was more often than not part of the duty solicitor scheme. Some officers would not give a full disclosure and would hold back some information in the hope that the suspect would be caught out in interview. This tactic is common when dealing with serious offences also. I had a habit, when I felt the case was a slam dunk, of disclosing as much as possible to solicitors in the hope that the defendant would see that the writing was on the wall and make a full and frank admission to their crime. This went better for them in regards to sentencing and brings into play options outside of court appearances such as restorative justice or cautions. However as this was a serious assault, and also domestic violence this would be going straight to the CPS (Crown prosecution Service) for a charging decision regardless of the defendant admitting the offences or otherwise. I was in a position to interview the suspect and put the matter to him, but unless he made a full confession I was not in a position to charge as I had not got at that point a formal complaint from the victim, or a detailed summary of her injuries.

This said on going through disclosure with the solicitor I pretty much knew what would happen during the interview. This was an unusual case in that there were witnesses who had both made statements and the victim was willing to make a full complaint and press charges. In this scenario the suspect only had two options; confess at the earliest opportunity or say nothing to prevent incriminating himself further. I left custody for a while as the suspect and his solicitor met to discuss his options.

The interview started at around 0200. All interviews begin by introducing everyone in the room, recording the time and date and giving the suspect details regarding his rights and entitlements. This done the suspect readily confirmed his name and date of birth.

I then arrested the suspect on suspicion of Section 18 GBH on tape and cautioned him. He confirmed he understood the caution and the reasons for this arrest. From that point on, his answer to every question I asked him was "No Comment". This is frustrating as it is like bashing your head against a brick wall, but you have to keep going. I had planned the interview carefully and kept firing questions at him, meeting the points I would have to prove to get him charged with GBH. As he answered each question "No Comment" I paused and asked him if her were sure. I reminded him that the advice given to him by his solicitor to go no comment was just that, advice and this was his opportunity to give his side of the story. I explained that should the matter go to court and he give an explanation for his actions there they would less likely to believe him as he had not used this chance to give an account. "No comment" repeated over and over. It is hard to keep this up, to be professional and keep going but there is no law against trying to get a comment out of him either. It is equally hard for him to continue to say nothing while being prompted and probed constantly. I threw in questions randomly such as "Do you enjoy beating woman" or "Did you mean to send her to hospital" followed up with "What do you feel about men who beat women?" I got one answer out of him this way by asking "Did you mean to hurt her so badly when you kicked and punched her?" to which he replied "No. I mean No Comment". It was my only chink of light but it did cause his solicitor to make an awful face. The interview lasted nearly an hour, which is a long time when you consider it was I throwing question after question at him and receiving two word answers.

You may wonder why would he go No comment like that? The answer was that without all the evidence being gathered there was a chance that the victim may decline to press charges, or there would be insufficient evidence. In that case to incriminate himself at that point may result in his being convicted anyway. Also if he could be bailed he had a chance to try and coerce the victim into dropping the case. I went away and compiled a summary of the interview before getting a package ready to go to the CPS. The CPS ran an out of hours service where I would fax the file to them, and remain on the telephone speaking to a lawyer and answering questions while they make a charging decision. It was a process that could take two or three hours for complex cases.

There was a tiny room set aside in Wisbech nick for this with a computer terminal, phone and fax machine. I went in, logged on and called the prosecutors. It took around an hour but the decision was to bail the suspect while further enquiries were conducted. I had hoped we could have charged him but as I still wanted the higher offence of GBH this was impossible. The further enquiries were to speak with the witnesses for more information, interview the victim for a detailed statement and obtain a complaint, and also get the victims authorisation to contact the hospital and her GP for a medical report on her injuries.

I went back to custody and briefed the custody Sergeant, who is on charge of the block and has to be fully informed. He was also responsible for authorising the bail conditions I wanted to set. I bailed "A" for a month to allow for enquiries to be made and he had conditions to not approach the victim in any way whatsoever, go within 200 metres of her home or contact either of the witnesses in any way. If he did any of those things he would be arrested.

I brought "A" in and bailed him. I then let him out of the police station to make his own way home. I then raised the crime of GBH, bringing all the actions I had taken up to date and recommending CID or the Domestic Violence unit take over, given the seriousness and nature of the assault. By the time I had finished it was time to go off duty, the case had taken me all eight hours of the shift to get this far.

I had a couple of rest days so arrived back on shift a day or so later and on booking on logged onto the computer to catch up on emails. All response officers carried their own crime queue of crimes that they were responsible for investigating such as minor thefts, assaults and other low-level offences. We were all trained to interview and investigate crimes but Detectives are trained to a higher degree for the more serious crimes. I found that I had been allocated the "A" and "H" case. I had also received an email from the DS who had told me well done for what I had done so far and carry on as per the CPS directions. I was glad. I was an experienced officer and I had investigated serious assaults before, and after a few days ruminating the events of that night I was ready to get medieval on "A" after he had gone "No Comment". If indeed he had committed this assault, "H" was getting the gold standard service and "A" was going to feel the full force of the law.

"H" was back at home after spending a day or so in Hospital, so I began by contacting her by phone and introducing myself as the Officer in the Case. I would be her point of contact from now on and I told her how to get in touch with me. We discussed what had happened briefly but the most disturbing thing that came from our conversation was that she was in abject terror of the suspect attacking her again. I made an appointment to see her at home later that day while I put certain other things in motion to try and safeguard her. I called the Domestic Violence unit and spoke to the officer for the Fenland area. We were at the time before DASH reports and detailed risk assessment of victims and pretty much everything was done ad hoc. I managed to secure a Jackpot alarm to be fitted to the victim's property, which was connected directly to the police. It consisted of a panic button which when pressed set off an alarm in the Force Control Room and immediate dispatch of officers to the house. On top of this I got hold of a police mobile telephone for the victim that she could use to call us in case of emergencies by pressing a single button. The number of this phone was recorded and the Force Control Room could do a search and identify the owner and send officers to her if she was not in a position to speak.

I went to see her later that day, and found a lady in a great deal of pain and psychological trauma. She had been released from hospital but did not quite know exactly what her injuries were; however she had been coughing up blood since and had seen her GP earlier that day. She did tell me that she had a condition with the Pancreas, which meant that direct violent trauma to the area could kill her, and that "A" knew this before the assault. She signed a form giving me her authority to get medical reports from both the hospital and her GP and I made an appointment to have the alarm fitted. I explained that "A" had bail conditions and what they were. "H" was at that point reluctant to make a formal complaint due to her fears of further attacks but after a long talk she agreed that I could come back the following day and take the statement from her. A slight concern at that point was that on hearing my name she connected me with my mum, who worked at the same place she did. She was happy as she had spoken to my mum who told her that her son was a brilliant officer (god love her) and she would be looked after. It was uncomfortable, as I did not want my personal or family life involved in my work at all. I asked "H" to not talk about the case in public and to please not try and pass messages to me through my mum. This was agreed.

I went away and sent copies of the consent form to the local GP and hospital. I also made further enquiries of the two witnesses who could not add further information. It was a waiting game until I got the medical reports, which would have the biggest bearing on what the charge would be.

Over the next week or so I was in regular contact with "H", she was extremely traumatised and nervous. She had an honest belief that "A" would come and get her. He had been seen outside her house on one occasion whilst I were off duty and arrested. Put before the next court he was let off with the same bail conditions. It's a frustrating business; he lived in the same village with his mother and argued he had to pass "H" house to get home. This caused still more trauma for "H" and I was in daily contact with her, as well as regularly patrolling the area myself. She even began referring to me as her 'personal policeman'. On my occasional visits she became more and more friendly and I became concerned she was seeing our relationship as something other than that of a police officer doing his job and supporting a victim of crime. This was borne out one day when I arrived following an alarm activation to reset the alarm, which was located in her bedroom. I reset the alarm and she was in the room. On her bed was laid out some very lacey nightwear that left little to the imagination. It was clear she wanted me to see it. I did not say anything about it, and left the house as soon as I could. I did not return, thankfully I was nearly ready to charge as the medical reports had come in. "H" was a vulnerable lady and I am sure she had allowed her heightened feelings escalate as she saw me as her protector. There was no infatuation or inappropriate behaviour but I felt it necessary to step back on order to stop any further feelings developing.

The medical evidence came in, detailing her injuries. "H" had suffered a bruised spleen, and very severe bruising to her ribs and exterior. She had escaped broken bones, so her injuries from a legal perspective were consistent with Actual Bodily Harm rather than Grievous Bodily Harm. The doctor had however confirmed that a heavy blow to her pancreas could well have proved fatal.

With this in mind I went back to the CPS with the file and a charge of ABH was authorised. I felt that "A" had got away with it, in that the lesser injuries he inflicted was by accident. He could have easily killed "H" and she deserved protection from the court. I charged "A" and he was bailed to attend court a few weeks later. What I had to do then was prepare the file in order for the CPS to have the fullest information to take into court. I went back to "H" for the final time and took a victim personal statement from her. This is a statement that the court can see and it tells them the impact that the crime has had on the victim. This one was explosive. I made sure "H" gave the full extent of the pain and trauma she had suffered. She had felt a prisoner in her own home and was afraid to go to work or leave the house. I then went to work on the file, making it as detailed and concise as I possibly could.

"A" had gone no comment in interview and never once showed remorse or admitted guilt. The Magistrates court decided almost immediately the despite the assault being that of ABH it did not have the power to sanction a penalty of adequate severity, balanced with the crime. A magistrate's court can only impose a prison sentence of up to six months. This meant that they thought a sentence of over six months was appropriate and they referred the case to the crown Court in Cambridge. It meant that "A" was out on bail again, but this time court bail instead of police bail, which meant a breach, was likely to see him remanded in Custody. He later received a long custodial sentence for his crime, and the case remains one of the most satisfying jobs I was part of during my service.

I never saw "H" again. I guess the release of the case being over and the safety it provided settled her down. "A" served around two years in prison and on his release was given an injunction preventing any contact with his victim.

Domestics really are the bread and butter policing that a front line officer deals with every day, and this is a sad fact. Over my career I must have attended hundreds of them and over time began to get really frustrated and ashamed of my fellow man for the terrible, childish and controlling behaviour they exhibited towards their victims. All too often I found myself dealing with identical scenarios with different victims and perpetrators. The following account is maybe the most extreme case of domestic abuse that I encountered from a psychological as well as physical aspect, and I feel it shows the lengths a desperate offender is willing to go to in order to continue the controlling behaviour he has displayed for years.

"C" was a very attractive mother of two. She had a seemingly happy marriage to people on the outside and looked like she was enjoying life, and raising her family in domestic bliss. I knew "C" from a distance outside of work, not to speak to but her children attended the same school as my daughter so I would see her in the playground. She was extremely attractive and always looked happy, well turned out and confident.

At the time I was the local Neighbourhood Constable for the town of March. As such I took an interest in all crime that happened in the town and where there was an ongoing issue such as harassment or ongoing domestic abuse I would often be tasked with taking ownership of the matter and seeing it through. Often I would pick up where another officer had left off and was rarely involved from the start, unless I was the first officer attending the initial report.

During shift one day I was tasked to attend a report of harassment. I went to the home address of the victim and was surprised to recognise "C" when she answered to door. "C" gave me an initial account of what had been going on, so that I was aware fully of the circumstances. Recently she had split up from her husband who I will call "D". Currently in progress was an investigation by the Domestic violence unit into abuse by "D" on "C" for almost the entire duration of the relationship, which was a significant period spanning a decade. It had been alleged that there was historical sexual abuse such as rape, and serious physical and mental abuse. The physical abuse included "D" beating "C" on a regular basis and also treating her as a slave, on occasions going so far as to urinate on her. This was as you can imagine extremely distressing for "C" to recount to me, and to be frank I am leaving much of it out here as it makes me sick to think about it. However, the investigation into these matters was going nowhere as "D" denied the abuse ever took place and there was no evidence that it had occurred. There had been no witnesses and the abuse had always been covert, in that "C" was controlled mentally. Contact with friends or family was curtailed and "D" controlled every aspect of her life. The law is an ass. It was plain through the demeanour of "C" that she was a victim of crime and abuse. She was nervous and guarded, and the subsequent behaviour of "D" eventually showed this. But the police were impotent at that time, as the CPS would never take the matter to court.

"C" had found the courage to end the marriage, which was a monumentally brave thing to do. "D" moved out and at first lived with his parents, but had suddenly rented a house that was situated literally at the end of "C's" garden. He had been harassing "C" in the form of text messages, phone calls and unannounced visits to the home for a period of several weeks but the move to a house so close to his victim was the straw that broke the camel's back for her. The nature of the calls, texts and visits was all the same. He wanted to resume the relationship, because he loved "C" and could not let her go. He had told "C" that he would never leave her and she should let him back into the house. He had made sexual advances and refused to take no for an answer. It was also obvious that he was stalking "C", turning up when she was out and about and having knowledge of her activities. The couple had children, both under ten. This was an important psychological lever for "D" as he had regular contact with them and to all intents and purposes was a diligent and loving father (he had never abused his children and they were not at risk from him). However the behaviour from "D" was escalating. He had got into the house while "C" was sleeping, watched her sleeping and changed her mobile phone so all text messages she sent or received were also copied to him. He had also damaged he satellite dish in the expectation she would call him to fix it.

Despite what she had been through, "C" was apologetic and felt she was wasting my time. I tried my best to let her know that nothing could be further from the truth. I assured her that I would help her and discussed the options available. I firstly advised her to change her mobile phone number, which would stop the texts arriving. From that point there were two routes available; firstly the civil route was to engage a solicitor to act on her behalf and take the matter to court to obtain a civil injunction against "D". Should a power of arrest be attached to it (Breaching such an order at that time was not arrestable and had to have the specific condition attached) she could call police and "D" could be arrested and put back before the court. The second option was the criminal route, whereby police gathered evidence and started the process of prosecuting "D" for harassment. The first step for this was for "D" to be issued a harassment warning. This was a document issued to him that he would sign which brought to his attention that an allegation of harassment had been made against him. Should he continue with his current course of conduct he could be arrested. It also states that the police at that time are not investigating or making a judgement on his guilt; the idea is to simply make him aware that the allegation has been made. It is very informal and no statements were taken from the victim at that time. It was essentially an attempt at a quick fix, which mostly worked. Most people take a waning such as this from a police officer seriously. I used to try and simplify it, by telling the offender that should I have to come back following another allegation the only reason for my returning would be to lock them up. In most instances these were issued to ex partners who were not dangerous, but would not take "no" for an answer. For most decent people a visit from the police is more than enough to make them realise their behaviour has been unreasonable.

After a lot of discussion with "C", she decided to go with the criminal route which is what I had recommended, as it quite frankly faster *'I would issue the warning immediately'* and cheaper *'It was free'*. I went to see "D", assuring "C" that I would update her as soon as I had seen him.

I literally only had to walk to the next street to find "D's" house and as I arrived at his front door I could see that the victims house could be seen from his front door.

"D" was home and I asked to come in which he agreed to. He worked as a carpet fitter, but "C" had told me his job was at stake as he had started drinking a lot and his obsessive behaviour had badly affected his work. His house was neat and tidy with the usual accoutrements that you would normally find in a single man's house, such as a big TV and games console.

I began to tell him why I was there, but felt he must have surely guessed. His reaction was extreme and took me by surprise. He began angrily, denying he was harassing anyone and only wanted to repair the relationship and make it all up to her. Then he calmed and became tearful, telling me he could not hurt her any more by leaving her. He was completely convinced his wife would take him back and he was doing her a favour of sorts by behaving like this. There was no mention about how "C" might feel, it was all about him. I had to bite my lip, but did tell him that "C" did not want him to contact her except through a solicitor or other third party to organise contact with the kids (who he declined to mention). I also listed the various things he had done, telling him I had read the texts and served the harassment notice to him. He signed, and undertook to stop his behaviour but I was in no doubt that I, or another officer would be returning. I had a sense that this was not the end of the matter and there were things going on that I and maybe even "C" did not know about. Basically "D" did not believe he was harassing "C" and that his actions showed that he loved her. He was deluded and very possibly mentally ill. At that point there was nothing I could do about it (And I had taken advice from a sergeant before leaving things as they were). I had followed the Domestic Violence and harassment policy correctly.

That done I went back to see "C", telling her that "D" had agreed to the notice and that he would stop contacting her. I also told her that should she have any problems she should ring 999 if she feels threatened and gave her the incident number to quote. On returning to the police station I made sure that I updated the incident and also had a domestic marker placed on "C's" address asking that all calls be treated as urgent. I also composed an email to the Domestic Violence unit, asking for them to organise an alarm for the house as "C" felt threatened and was unsure as to whether "D" still had a key (I had advised her to change the locks). I had also completed a DV risk assessment of "C" and had made her high risk of further abuse or harm. Finally I made a note on the briefing system to ensure all local officers knew of the issue and would give due attention should there be further calls. I had a feeling that this was a journey that would not end well. I commented at the time to DV unit I felt that C and indeed D were at risk.

A couple of days passed with no incident. However I was on duty on the third day or so when there was an "A" grade incident for "C's" address. "D" had arrived at the address intoxicated and had thrown a can of food (I can't remember what exactly) through the back window of "C's" car. I and other officer's blue lighted to the scene to find "D" had gone. However "C" remained in an understandably shocked and frightened state. It transpired that there had been more harassment that she had not immediately reported over the past couple of days. "C" had changed her phone number as suggested, but somehow "D" had got hold of it. He had also found some way of getting all the texts that "C" sent or received also sent to his own phone. He had told "C" that he knew what she was doing and who she had been talking to, going into detail as to what the contents of text messages to her were. The only way he could have done this was to actually have contact with "C's" phone, which was disturbing. "C" had also noticed that things had been moved in the house, and that the satellite dish at the back of the house was out of place, suggesting he had been inside. But what disturbed me the most was that "C" reported the only time her phone was actually out of her control was when she was asleep, and the phone was charging beside her bed. This meant that if "D" had actually got hold of it he had been in "C's" bedroom while she slept. It was a bit spine chilling if those were the lengths he was willing to go to in order to control and monitor her.

Another officer stayed with "C" to take a statement from her, which included a formal complaint for the criminal damage as well as detailed information regarding the harassment. I went to make the arrest.

"D" had not gone far. He had gone home and must have known we would be paying him a visit. He admitted fully causing the damage but was shocked and surprised when I also arrested him for harassment. He was genuinely in denial and kept repeating "I can't do that to her". He was also falling down drunk.

I took him into custody and booked him in. As part of the process I had to document him which meant taking his fingerprints, photograph and a DNA sample. It took a long time as he was intoxicated, but also he could not stop talking about "C". He spoke about their marriage in the present tense; not believing it was over. Constantly he repeated "I can't do it to her" in the context that he could not hurt her by leaving her. He also displayed a lot of guilt regarding his treatment of her. Repeated over and over again was his belief that he could not live without her and she without him. It was obsessive behaviour I had certainly not experienced before. He was constantly in floods of tears and was in genuine anguish, which I believed was fuelled as much by his own guilt as well as the obsession he was suffering from. "D" had been an abuser of the foulest kind for many years, but he could not bring himself to leave "C" alone and was in a genuine and severe depression. He made dozens of comments regarding his lack of will to live, as well as the love he felt "C" still felt for him and I was certain that if this was not handled well the whole thing would result in either a suicide, or a murder. He was under caution and everything he said would be treated as 'significant statements' and these would be used as evidence and put to him in interview. He would not however be interviewed for some hours as he would not be sober enough for a long time, certainly after I had gone off duty. I did manage to get a police surgeon (on call Doctor) out to examine him with a view to getting his assessed by the mental health team. I hoped that he could be sectioned and if treated would get his life back on track and face his crimes head on.

I completed a handover package for the as yet unidentified officer who would conduct the interview, making sure that all the comments made were recorded. The evidence that we had in the form of copies of text messages, "C's" statement, and the significant comments made by "D" I felt ensured that he would be charged; but it was the safeguarding of the victim that I was the most concerned with. I made sure I had provided a detailed update to the DV unit, who had already taken the case on, at my first involvement. I made it clear that both parties were at risk and that "D" needed to be dealt with as soon as possible.

I retired from duty and on my next shift found that "D" had been charged and bailed to court. He had strict bail conditions not to contact "C" directly or indirectly and to not attend her house. A doctor had attended but had not agreed that "D" needed help with his immediate mental health.

"D" did go on to breach his bail by further contacting "C". He was arrested on I believe two occasions (I was not involved in this) and on each occasion was granted bail again by the court. However he then stopped and I hoped that he would now get the matter settled in court and eventually get on with his life. I had no further day to day involvement, as the case was now with the DV unit so received no other update. The final part of this tale was a tragic end. I was not involved as I was off duty, but I heard the tale afterwards from the officers that did. "D" again began to contact "C" stating he was going to commit suicide. He had done this many times before and never harmed himself. Over the day several texts were sent which "C" ignored, but stored on her phone, however eventually she received a final goodbye. She called the police to report the texts, but also to express her concern for "D". He had abused and hurt her for a long time and frankly made her life hell, but love is an emotion that cannot just be forgotten. Out of concern C went to D's address and found he had hung himself from the loft hatch. He had hung himself immediately after sending the final text to "C", deliberately planning that she would be the one to find him, a final terrible act of control and abuse. There was nothing anyone could have done in the end to prevent this, short of actually locking "D" up. It was a tragically sad end to a terrible period for all concerned. I will not try and guess how and why this scenario ended up costing someone their life, but I do feel that it could have been prevented. I will let the reader decide.

There is not much to add following this story. However I did think deeply about the incident and concluded that there was nothing more I could have done while I was involved. There was an investigation and inquest into "D's" death, which absolved the police of any negligence. What stands out to me now was during the time I spent in custody with "D", he did not mention his children once. It was a powerful reminder of the power of obsessive love.

This will be my final account of a domestic violence incident. It is a subject I have not enjoyed writing about and one that is still a sickening and horrible thing. I have not been involved in a case that has resulted in murder, but a large proportion of murders are committed within relationships. The incident I will now refer to did not end in a murder; however the level of physical torture that was inflicted was serious and undoubtedly would have resulted in the eventual death of the victim.

Wisbech is jokingly called Wisbekistan by many local people because of the high proportion (around a third of the population) being of Eastern European origin. I will talk about this group in greater detail later in the book so will now say little about them. What I will say is that in the main they are honest hard working people who have moved to the UK to improve their lives and the lives of their family.

I was working a late shift at Wisbech in 2012, where I was posted as a reactive constable. A job came in on Norwich Road stating a domestic was in progress. A very distressed and agitated Eastern European Woman was being harassed or assaulted by an Eastern European male. I did not attend the scene originally but other members of my shift did.

What followed was the arrest of a Russian male, initially for assault I believe. A woman of Lithuanian origin had been taken to hospital by ambulance, with injuries described by my sergeant as "The worst I have ever seen on a person who is still alive and conscious".

Several officers had been to the scene and arrested the perpetrator. This meant that they could not speak to or have any contact with the victim due to cross contamination issues. Basically the rule is if you have had contact with a suspect you cannot have contact with the victim due to the possibility of forensic evidence being passed between them. An example of this is rape. Contact with the suspect could transfer fibres from clothing or DNA onto the officer who can then transfer that material onto the victim. The risk of such cross contamination can destroy a prosecution in the same manner that the trial of Barry George (who was acquitted on appeal for the murder of TV presenter Jill Dando).

I was the only officer not attached to the incident so I was sent to the hospital to see the victim who I located in Accident and Emergency. The victim "Z" could not speak English very well and was waiting to be seen by a doctor. She was being comforted by a ward janitor who was also Lithuanian and could speak to her. What I first noticed was that "Z" had terrible burn marks all up her arms, on her face and legs. If you have never seen a cigarette burn they are not hard to spot and these were livid, in differing states of healing everywhere. There must have been fifty or so of them everywhere. Disgusting. "Z" was also in really bad pain, moving gingerly with visible bruises turning her skin violet all over her arms, face and back. She was a very slight slim lady, which made her injuries look even worse. She was also in a very emaciated state, certainly she had lost a lot of weight quickly. I realised that the Sergeant had not exaggerated when she described the injuries as the worst she had seen on a live person.

"Z" was hungry, and the hospital provided her with sandwiches. She ate one packet after another and must have eaten six of them. At this point I will mention that her breath was terrible. I did not comment on it, as I doubted that oral hygiene was at the top of anyone's agenda but I identified the odour which is associated with malnourishment as the body uses its reserves to keep going. Through the interpreter I began to explain who I was, and why I was there. "Z" was terrified of me, simply because I was a man. She had been through about as much suffering as it was possible to go through, as I was to eventually find. I had to fill in a sexual offence booklet, which was a first account from a victim of what has happened to them. It was a long time however before I could start to do this, "Z" was incredibly nervous and I had to at least gain her trust, or at least reassure her she was now safe. That was my goal. I told "Z" she was safe, that it was over, and I was going to make sure that she was looked after. She did not believe me at first, her ordeal was so severe that she was still in the midst of the terror and pain she had suffered. She told me what a nice man I seemed, but really she did not believe that such a thing existed. It was very sad. It was a couple of hours of just general chatting before she began to open up and tell me some of what had happened.

The man arrested was her partner and they lived together. She had been locked in a toilet without food or fresh water for a fortnight. She had been reduced to drinking from the toilet, as the taps did not work. She had not eaten at all for two weeks. A nurse explained to me that this explained her bad breath, as it was a symptom of starvation. When the body is not getting food it begins to eat itself, in that the body uses fat reserves to maintain itself explaining the weight loss. This in turn creates the enzymes in the gut, which produce the odour. Poor lady. And it certainly explained why she was eating the horrible Hospital sandwiches like they had gone out of fashion!

"Z" had been abused in every way imaginable. She had been repeatedly beaten, sometimes into unconsciousness. She had been burned with cigarettes countless times. She had also been raped, anally, vaginally and orally on multiple occasions (too many for her to count or remember). She had been used as a slave. Actually worse than that. She had been starved and abused in a way that was unimaginable. Other than the physical effects the mental side was obviously going to take her months or years to recover from, if she did at all. She had managed to escape, using the last of her strength when in his drunken state the suspect had left the bathroom unlocked in error and fallen asleep. I relayed this information to the Detective Sergeant who had taken the job on. My shift mates were gathering the evidence at the scene and booking the suspect in to custody.

I told her again that she was safe. It was over. The man who had done this was in police custody and could not hurt her again. Finally her body language told me that she believed me. Her shoulders visibly relaxed a little and the sudden realisation caused her to break down. She only said two words to me "thank you". It was enough. I completed the booklet, which was a simple first account of what happened. It did not need any detail other than a very rough outline. I had to explain to "Z" that another officer, who would be a lady if she preferred, would interview her when she felt stronger and obtain a full account. She would also be examined by a doctor to gather evidence and this would be rather personal. She nodded. She had been through hell and her ordeal was not going to be over fully just yet if we wanted to get justice for her.

"Z" was taken away to have x-rays as it seemed impossible that her external injuries would not translate into broken bones. That was the kicker. When the X-rays came back it was revealed that "Z" had a broken back and a fractured skull.

I did not see or speak to the suspect at all. And when I left the hospital I did not have any further involvement in the case, which was taken on by CID. However from my shift colleagues I found out what happened. The suspect was taken to hospital himself some hours after his arrest. The reason for this was alcohol poisoning. He was in hospital for three days before he was released due to his withdrawing from alcohol. He had basically been drunk constantly for weeks. He was taken back to custody and was eventually interviewed. He was charged for multiple rapes, GBH, and false imprisonment amongst other things. He laughed when he was charged. He showed no remorse. Pure evil.

"Z" recovered. She was released from hospital but I do not know what became of her. Her abuser who I do not wish to dignify with even a fake name was sent to prison for a long time. On his release he will be deported back to Russia and will never be allowed to enter the country again. What stands out is that if "Z" had not had the presence of mind to escape she would have died. I am personally pleased that we as a service were able to put the perpetrator away, but on his return to Russia I am doubtful that he will not re-offend. I guess we will never find out.

CHAPTER 9 – MISSSING PERSONS

Missing persons in the main are incidents that are resolved quite quickly. A very high percentage of reports of missing people to police are routine; for example children in care. That's not to say that children in care are not vulnerable; they certainly are. However because they are under care orders the staff in care homes are required to call the police when they are missing, even if they are a few minutes late home. Many of these young people are also very streetwise and will do what they want regardless of what their care order says. It is very rare that they come to harm and they mostly return in their own good time. Even when located by police they will often run away or just abscond again the following day. It was frustrating because as a police officer I wanted to safeguard them, but in the end it was a waste of police time looking for a young person who was either not going to be found unless they wanted us to, or care staff were actually sitting back and asking us to do their job for them. Every town has regular missing persons from local authority care homes and the hangouts of all of them are well known.

Other missing persons (such as the story of "L" in the Suicide Chapter) jump out at you from the onset as serious incidents that need a lot of attention immediately. One such instance I was involved in (in a very limited capacity) is arguably still the highest profile missing person's enquiry ever seen in this country. It was a search, and later a manhunt that united a community and captured the whole nation, and disgusts anyone who remembers it to this day. A story of two girls who were murdered by a sick man who was protected by his partner. Of course I am talking about operation Fincham; Soham. The story of Holly Wells and Jessica Chapman, and it sends chills down my spine just typing the words.

Firstly I would like to say that my involvement in what became Operation Fincham was limited, in that I was not a police officer when it happened. I was at the time working as a civilian in the control room and on the night of Sunday the 4th August 2002 was on the Cambridge Radio terminal. I was the dispatcher for the Cambridge City area as well as the towns around it, including Ely (of which Soham is a part). I knew Soham fairly well and had visited on several occasions socialising with friends who lived in the town. It is a small town with a strong community feel, everyone knows everyone else.

What happens in the force control room is quite simple really. Calls come in either via the 999 system or the non-emergency line, which are answered by call takers who create an incident on the command and control system, graded in order of priority and sent to the relevant dispatch terminal for action. At the time the highest grade was 'A' grade which was a blue light response, going down to B grade (within and hour), C Grade (as and when) and D grade (we don't attend at all).

It was around 2000 and I was on a 1700 – 0200 shift. I had just taken over the radio for a colleague who had gone for their meal break. A missing from home incident on a "B" grade was transferred to my terminal from a call taker. It was a call from the parents of two ten year old girls. Daughters from two families, Jessica Chapman and Holly Wells had been missing for a couple of hours. They had gone out to buy sweets and despite a search by the families they had not been found. Jessica also had a pay as you go mobile phone but this was not connecting either. The girls were both 10 years old. Obviously this was an incident that had to be treated with some urgency and I dispatched an officer from Ely Police Station to attend immediately. He arrived a short time afterwards and had been at the house for around 10 minutes when he excused himself and went to another room. Calling up over the radio he told me "There is something not right here. I am very worried about these girls". Following this, things snowballed. I contacted the duty sergeant for the area and also advised the dispatch supervisor in the control room that this incident was ongoing. From here it all began. By the time the officer arrived the community was starting to turn out to search, word had spread and by the time midnight came round there were literally hundreds of people out and about searching for Holly and Jessica. There were not many resources on the ground on that first night, as many officers as possible were drafted in from around the division and police began to organise the public volunteers so that a systematic search of the town could be begun.

I offered to stay on and work overtime but at that time I was not needed. I went home reluctantly at 0200. The next morning I woke up early and on turning on the TV found that the little town of Soham had become national news. It seemed that the media had descended on the town overnight and a search on a massive scale was underway. From a police perspective the machine had also started moving, officers were brought in from neighbouring counties and detectives were also starting to investigate the girl's disappearance. Members of the public were being spoken to and interviewed, one of which was one Ian Huntley, caretaker of the local school who as it turned out was one of the last people to have seen the girls. Other resources such as detectives from the Millie Dowler case were brought in and a specialist bloodhound was summoned from Wales to try and pick up their trail. For every second that ticked away, it was less likely that there was going to be a happy ending.

I wanted to help in any limited way I could. Colleagues of mine in the control room were Special Constables, and many of them volunteered to go over and help with the search. I was not able to do this. However as the profile of Holly and Jessica's disappearance increased, so did the calls from the general public offering information or help. An incident room was set up in the Major Operations Room, known as the MOR. The MOR was a room adjoining the Force Control Room fitted out with terminals, telephones and the Gold Room, essentially an office for senior officers. The MOR was only opened for major incidents, and on this occasion it was used as an incident room where calls from the public offering information or making enquiries would be directed. A telephone number for the public to call was established and it went from there. I worked numerous shifts in the incident room. Calls came in from all over the world and I probably spoke to several hundred people over the course of a fortnight. They ranged from what a lot of people would call crackpots, people who said they were mediums, or dowsers who had experienced visions. One call that stuck in my mind was from a Christian group who had been praying and one of them had received a vision. They told me they had seen a detached house with a red door and thought it was connected. Its easily to dismiss these things as the ramblings of attention seekers or lunatics but these people were sincere, and had an honest belief that God had sent them the vison. There were so many of these types of calls that they melted into each other. It was hard to remain polite and take each call seriously, and the people were not to know that hundreds of other psychics, mediums and the like had called in. They all said the same things on a different level, be it a vision of a house or woods, or a school. It is hard to take it seriously but at that stage you rule nothing out.

However other calls came through from people who were not claiming to have some kind of divine vision. For instance David Beckham was rumoured to have contacted the police to offer his help in some sort of appeal; both girls had been wearing Manchester united shirts with his name on the back. Other members of the public called offering to travel from all over the country to help search (which was after a while discouraged as the operation took shape). A frequent theme however was a clear suspicion from the community, and others around the country regarding Ian Huntley. Huntley had appeared on television describing how awful he felt about being one of the last people to see the girls, and how distressing it all was for the community. Something in his tone and body language put people on edge; there were many calls just stating "You should have a good look at that caretaker". One call even accused him of being a sex offender previously in Grimsby. Members of the community also called in to tell us that they thought he was responsible. I in fact ran him through the Police national Computer myself after such a call. He had a police record on there, but no convictions; which was odd. It was common with very old records where a conviction had become obsolete, or someone had been found not guilty of an offence. The errors in the checking of Huntley were later uncovered in a review with Humberside and Cambridgeshire Police Forces, and the deaths of the girls in part has helped such things never happening again.

Some calls were of course potential sightings of the girls. These were followed up as and when they came in but rarely did anything seem concrete enough to actually be a reliable sighting. As it turns out of course none of the sightings were real. The force had utilised a computer programmed called HOLMES, which was a system that collated and presented evidence as and when it emerged. It is a tool that was widespread amongst the whole force nation-wide as a tool in the investigation of serious crime. Whenever a call came in it was recorded on a database, which was reviewed by the detective's investigation what became a murder enquiry. The more urgent looking pieces of information were printed and physically taken to the HOLMES team.

I, and I have to say most colleagues I encountered during the time between the girl's disappearance up until their bodies were found had an honestly held belief that we would find them safe and well. So many people in the control room worked ceaselessly in the MOR, working 16 and 18 hour shifts before coming back a few hours later to do another. We were all mothers or fathers in our own lives and just wanted to help and find those kids. It was soul destroying as the days went by and no sign of them was found. One night I was in the MOR when both sets of parents came in to see what was happening in there; they even listened in to some of the calls. I felt a deep sympathy and compassion for them as a parent myself and could not even comprehend the terrible worry that was going through their minds.

On the day that the bodies were found there was anguish among everyone. Such a sad day. When the news that Huntley had been arrested along with his partner Maxine Carr no one was surprised. It turns out he had indeed been a suspect from the start and detectives had deployed a whole raft of surveillance on him and Carr. Jessica's last known location when it was switched off was triangulated to a location very close to his house and Carr had also lied about her location that weekend. Tactics were used to try and put pressure on Huntley to make him crack and make a mistake and he was interviewed informally by detectives several times prior to his arrest. Even after his arrest he was calm and cool, eventually frothing at the mouth and talking gibberish to convince people he was insane. Carr also never turned on him and stuck to her story. Vitally it was physical evidence that convicted Huntley. The remains of the girls shirts were found hidden in a bin within the school Huntley was a caretaker at and his fingerprints were on the bin bag they were hidden beneath. In addition he had tripped up to one of my colleagues working as a Special Constable during the search. He queried about the destruction of DNA evidence and the only reliable method being fire. My colleague gave evidence during the trial to this effect. As it turns out the girls had already been murdered by Huntley by the time police were called in. He had killed them in his bathroom, and then tried to destroy their tiny bodies by burning them in the school furnace. The bodies when found had no evidence on them as he had destroyed it, along with their bodies, which were described by HM Pathologist Nat Carey as partially skeletonised. The sick twisted bastard had even robbed the families of the chance to see their faces one last time. Carr's lies about where she was at the time of the murders were also uncovered. She had claimed to be in Soham with Huntley; thus providing an alibi but phone analysis proved she was in Grimsby.

Huntley was sent to prison and I hope he rots there. He tried from the point of arrest to look insane, foaming at the mouth and babbling incoherently and carried this behaviour through several days of questioning before he was sent to Rampton Secure Hospital. It did him no good as he was found to be fit to stand trial. He was never charged with any form of sexual assault as any possible evidence of such a crime had been destroyed when he semi cremated the bodies. The trial judge when passing sentence stated that sexual assaults were likely but not provable, and this was the main reason Huntley escaped a full life tariff.

I remember the day of the first court appearance at Peterborough Magistrates. Afterwards the officers involved walked along the road and were cheered by the hundreds of people who had turned up. It was a proud moment for the team and richly deserved. One of these officers was Brian Stevens who was the family liaison officer for the family of Jessica Chapman, and spent almost the entire enquiry by their side. He had won the trust of the family and was asked to read a poem at Ely Cathedral on the occasion of the service celebrating Holly and Jessica's life as a mark off that trust.

Shortly after the trial of Huntley, Stevens was arrested and charged with having indecent images of children on his laptop. At trial the case collapsed on a technicality, as a witness had stated Stevens was with her when the images were downloaded and he was not the only person who had access to the laptop. Acquitted of this, Stevens was then arrested three weeks later and sent to prison for eight months for perverting the course of justice. His alibi was fabricated. I came across him after I had joined the police force (He had been sacked himself of course). I caught him committing two driving offences that were reasonably minor (speeding and overtaking over a double white line). I stopped him and reported him for the offences, sending him to court. I remember him commenting that it was a bit harsh. Yes it was. He deserved it.

Huntley to this day has never apologised or showed remorse for the murder of little Holly and Jessica. After the trial it emerged that he had been investigated on numerous occasions for sexual offences on children under 16, one of which was against an 11-year-old. The only time he was charged was for a rape on an adult but the CPS dropped the case. An inquiry was ordered by the Home Secretary to discover the reason this man managed to get a job at a school. A tape was found in his cell that contained his confessions to various offences and he has been attacked in Prison twice and in addition has attempted to take his own life twice. Carr served nearly two years of a prison sentence for attempting to pervert the course of justice and was given plastic surgery to change her appearance prior to her release. She has carried on her life. It is rumoured she held a job in Spalding at Morrison's working the night shift until she revealed who she was to a colleague. She was immediately got rid of, by her colleagues. I have no idea what has become of her, and frankly I don't care. I know she did not kill those girls, but she tried to protect Huntley, and refused to denounce him. That makes her as guilty as him in my mind. She has a lifelong

injunction that extends to a child she gave birth to in recent years, which means the

child will never know who her mother was.

The year following the case myself and my now ex-wife had a little girl ourselves, who

we named Jessica; mostly because we loved the name but also as a small tribute to

one of the little girls who would never see another birthday. RIP Holly and Jessica.

You will never be forgotten.

CHAPTER 10 – SPILLS, ASSAULTS, OUCHY!

Assaults are again, bread and butter for the reactive constable. The severity of assaults range significantly; from common assaults where the injuries are non-existent or very slight, right up to GBH and Murder. Serious assaults are dealt with of course by detectives and in the case of Murder Senior officers who are experienced and seasoned in these types of crime. However the initial officers attending reports of assault are almost always reactive officers, responding to the first 999 call from the public. This of course means that officers deal with and investigate hundreds of assaults every year.

I am pretty certain that there is not an officer anywhere who has never been assaulted. It is a shame that these days courts do not treat the assault on a police officer as seriously as they used to. Once upon a time if you assaulted a police officer you faced prison, but nowadays if there are other offences connected to it such as a burglary it is common for little deals to be made and the assault to be dropped, if the defendant pleads guilty to another offence (if the assault is minor). With the pressures that Police now face, assaults are on the increase and there have been some very real and tragic deaths of police officers over recent years in the course of their duty.

As a police officer I was assaulted on numerous occasions but was fortunate that none of the assaults resulted in serious injury. One quick story I would like to account is an assault on me one Saturday night in March. It concerns a 'lady' I will call "X". She was an alcoholic, or at the very least a heavy drinker and was a woman of a certain age, in her late forties. She was heavy set and had a real reputation as being game and eager to throw punches. She was known to have beaten up several people, men included. One night I was on patrol when I was called to a local club.

The bouncer, who was black, had called to report an assault on him by a female who had also racially abused him, calling him a "Black Bastard". Arriving at the scene I found "X" who was drunk and shouting at anyone nearby. Speaking to the victim I learned "X" had tried to get into the club and had been refused entry due to her intoxication. In a fit of rage she had punched the bouncer (Who was around 6 ft 8 inches tall and built like a brick outhouse) and racially abused him. After confirming that he wanted to make a complaint I with my colleague approached her and I quickly arrested her for racially aggravated common assault and applied handcuffs to her, behind her back. Through my advising her she was under arrest and cautioning her she shouted and swore at me, calling colourful names such as Pig, Cunt and Shithead. Lovely lady who obviously completed finishing school! This was in a public place in the middle of town so I further arrested her for Section 5 public order act, which is basically abusive behaviour in a public place. We put her in the back of the police car, but decided she was far too volatile to be taken all the way to Wisbech in a car. We needed a van with a cell in the back to transport her safely. As I have said "X" had a reputation around the town and to be honest it was not unfounded. But when she had not had a drink she was a sweetheart, very approachable, friendly and essentially non-violent. However when drunk she was able to give anyone a hiding be they male or female, big or small. I radioed asking for a van, and sods law the nearest one was miles away and would take 20 minutes to arrive. We left "X" in the rear of the car where no one could hear her shouting and kept an eye on her.

It was not long before "X began complaining that her cuffs were too tight. I opened the door and checked them, making sure they were not tight (however they are not designed for comfort). I explained this to "X" and closed the door. "X" began shouting louder and louder that the cuffs were too tight, so my colleague checked them also and was satisfied that they were all OK. "X" then rolled onto her back on the seat of the car and began systematically kicking the windows with the soles of her feet (thankfully she had taken her high heels off). She screamed and foamed at the mouth while she did this. We opened the car door to prevent this and removed her from the car. Standing there between the two of us she began to kick out again, this time in the direction of my testicles. She missed thankfully. At this point we applied leg restraints to her legs. Leg restraints are lengths of canvass about two inches across which have Velcro on them. You used two of these, one around the ankles and one above the knees to prevent a person kicking out or to help subdue someone who was resisting, they cause no pain and cause no damage. Once you have these on you have to have someone holding onto you to prevent you from falling over. I was helping to hold "X" up and she was shouting and swearing at me. I ignored her, other than telling her that she was just making things worse for herself and pointed out the CCTV cameras that were recording everything we did.

Without warning "X" turned towards me and spat full in my face. I was speaking as she did this and her saliva went into my mouth and eyes and dribbled down my cheek. It was disgusting – a right loogy! Many a copper will tell you they would rather get a punch in the face than be spat at and I was in full agreement. There is obviously a worry of infection as well as the fact it is simply disgusting and repugnant.

I did not react other than telling "X" she was further under arrest for assault on Police and reminding her she was still under caution. Her reply was "fuck off". Classy lady. She looked like she was going to spit again, so we applied the final thing to prevent this from happening. Quite recently the spit hood had been introduced for just such an incident and we had only been issued with them recently. A spit hood is a paper bag with black mesh to the front, which you put over someone's head to cover his or her face. When they have it on they cannot see very well but obviously they cannot spit at you either. I applied one of these to "X". No more spitting (although there was an increase in the shouting and swearing which now reached an ear splitting finale).

Finally a van turned up and took her away to custody. The Prisoner Handling Team would deal her with the following morning.

It will come as no surprise that "X" was charged with racially aggravated assault as well as assault on me. A few weeks later I and the other officers who were there were summoned to court to give evidence, as X had pleaded not guilty. We all waited our turn before going in and swearing the oath. My time on the stand lasted about 30 minutes and I found the defence solicitor's attempts at tripping me up highly amusing. There were lots of questions that started with "I put it to you officer….". I remained calm and told the truth. I then went to sit in the public gallery and watched some of my colleagues giving evidence. The defence solicitor was obviously trying to get his client off with assaulting me (The bouncer had not turned up at court so the charges would be dropped). One officer "R" when asked how could he be sure "X" Spat at me simply said, "I saw the saliva flying through the air from the mouth of X. I then saw it dribbling down PC Rudd's face". He said it in such a dead pan way I had to stifle a laugh.

The magistrates did not take long to come back and find "X" guilty of assault against a police officer. On hearing this, her comment was "Why am I not surprised?". She was given a community order and also had to pay £50 to me in compensation. She did this very quickly which was surprising, A lot of officers get compensation awarded and receive it in instalments of tiny proportions. Sums of fifty pence a week are not uncommon. A lot of Bobbies don't even bank the cheques. I did. I think I spent most of it on Mouthwash!

A couple of weeks after this was in court I was pulled into the office by an Inspector, who worked with PSD. He issued me with a regulation 9 notice, which was basically a tool to tell me I was being investigated for misconduct. Basically "X" had made a complaint that I had used excessive force on her! I was surprised to say the least but the Inspector went to great pains to tell me it was nothing to worry about and no decent police officer goes through life without getting a complaint or two. At the time I only had about two years in service so went with the flow, but firmly thought I had used force that was appropriate and proportionate in the circumstances. "X" has been arrested for assault and handcuffed, she had tried to kick the windows of the police car out so had leg restraints applied, and finally she had spat at me so had a spit hood applied. Perfectly reasonable in the circumstances I thought. I was very surprised to have a local resolution form put in front of me to sign. I was told that was the end of the matter and did not know it meant I was admitting liability. I was done over and later regretted signing it. It was the same inspector that issued the Reg 9 notice, and I was annoyed that despite the promise that the force would stand up for me, I had been coerced into signing a form that indicated I accepted a local resolution. This was (and I did not know at the time) a disciplinary resolution that would remain on my file for the duration of my career. It was my first personal experience of PSD, and the underhand way in which they did things. I was to learn much more later.

The next assault I will describe to you, was the most serious crime I ever arrested someone for: Attempted Murder. One Sunday afternoon I was on duty in March, when a call came out over the radio asking for officers to attend a domestic dispute in a tiny village called Pondersbridge, located right on the edge of our sector the other side of Whittlesey. I was in March and blue lit to the scene which took 20 – 30 minutes due to the remote location of the village. Arriving at the scene I found a male in his twenties with a gaping wound on the top of his head, cradling a crate of lager. He was very animated and excited (and more than a little drunk). He sat on the kerb outside the location of the incident, which was a small bungalow. Opening another can of beer he told me that he had an argument with his stepfather which had ended with his stepfather hitting him over the top of the head with a shovel. The injury to the top of his head was serious and there was a flap of skin with his hair on it blowing around in the breeze! The male who I will call "J" did not seem to care, despite the blood seeping out of the wound and down the back of his head. He was worried about his mother who was still in the house and he stated that his stepfather had knocked her about in the past. I did not know "J", and took what he said at face value. He also told me that his stepfather meant to kill him and had told him so when he hit him.

Before I could do anything else a small dog ran out of the front gate which "J" had left open and ran across the road into the yard of a large shed or barn. "J" chased it as he wanted to get it back into the house and I followed. I radioed the current situation to the control room and another officer arrived; Dave. Dave was a medic and his skills were definitely required as when we got across the road and found "J" he suddenly collapsed and began fitting violently on the ground. This was a disturbing scenario and it looked very serious for "J". I remember radioing for an Ambulance as soon as possible and commenting that we could be losing the witness. Dave took over his care and waited for the Ambulance and I went back over the road where other officers had arrived. I had no physical contact with "J" so was not in danger of any cross contamination.

A team of around four of us then knocked on the door and found the lady of the house who was "J's" mother. She confirmed that there had been an assault but stated her husband had left the house.

Some officers remained inside to perform a search and I and another officer went outside and bumped into the suspect in the side garden. I promptly arrested him on suspicion of attempted murder and cautioned him. We waited for a van and took him through to custody where I booked him in, seized his clothing and completed a handover package. The spade used was also found and brought in as evidence.

CID took over from that point, and did not like the fact that I had arrested for attempted murder. From my point of view I had reasonable suspicion that the suspect had intended to kill "J" when he hit him over the head with a spade, he had even said as much as he did it. The managers did not want an Attempted murder on the books, simple as that, so the eventual charge was for Section 20 GBH.

Months passed until it went to court and I was called as a witness. The trial was held at Cambridge Crown court and was pencilled in for five days. The first day was spent sitting around doing nothing as we waited for things to get started. Trials always take a long time to get going, mainly as the CPS and defence gets together and have little discussions to try and get deals done before they get into court. It saves time of course but I don't like the game playing aspect of it. More often than not a defendant will go not guilty all the way up to the hearing just waiting to see if all the witnesses turn up. If they do they will enter an early guilty plea and get a reduced sentence; if they don't they stand a good chance of the case collapsing and getting off so continue to protest their innocence.

On this occasion the main witness "J" did turn up. He had survived the attack but apparently still had fits as he had sustained a brain injury. It was a surprise that he had shown up as it turned out he was himself well known to police and a known heroin user. However he was there, dressed smartly and looking like a good and reliable witness.

I was called into the witness box on the second day. I was not there long. I was asked by the prosecution to simply read my statement in open court, and the defence declined to cross-examine me. This indicated that my statement was good, and there were no holes in it for the defence to exploit. I rarely had to spend too long in the witness box at any trial as I always tried to be as detailed as possible in my statement. It was a tip I had picked up over my time and it served me well. When you give evidence you can always have your statement and pocket notebook with you to refresh your memory, and if you have your notes right no one can really dispute your honesty, even if they choose to not believe you.

I did not follow any more of the trial and was back on normal duty the following day. The defendant was found guilty of GBH and sentenced accordingly.

"J" despite being a drug user prior to this event was a reliable and credible witness. I heard he moved to the south coast with his partner and turned his life around, getting himself free of drugs.

The final assault I will describe is a serious assault that happened in March on St Patrick's day 2011. It was significant to me as at the time Television cameras were filming a fly on the wall documentary about Cambridgeshire constabulary called

"Cop Squad". My involvement in this incident ended up being televised which was a nice thing my myself and my family.

The incident predictably occurred in a Town centre pub, one known for hard drinkers to frequent. There had been a skirmish within which resulted in the offender punching another man to the face, causing him to fall backwards and hit his head. As I arrived at the police station he was in cardiac arrest and being treated by the Ambulance service. In short at that time we had a potential murder on our hands.

There were already officers at the scene so I was not needed. However my role was to take the form of an advisor of sorts, as my knowledge of the suspect and his family was detailed.

"P" was a man in his forties who I had known all my life, as I had grown up around the corner from him. He was married and had around 10 children, living in an ex council house on an estate. As well as the children he had a large number of dogs, Rottweilers and German Shepherds. He was well known to the police and I had arrested him myself a couple of years before for entering a pub with a big tyre iron in his back pocket that he had intended to clump someone around the head with. He was thick set, tough and potentially dangerous as well as being a cocaine user (and suspected dealer). He was on a suspended sentence for a sexual assault on a 12 year old girl and a vicious assault outside a job centre where he punched a woman in the face. He had escaped gaol due to his having to care for ten children but had been warned by the Judge that he would not be shown the same mercy again.

While we were gathering at the police station I found the cameras seeking me out and I had to do a "piece" to camera about what we were going to do. I explained that we were dealing with a potential murder and it was important that we detained the suspect safely and quickly in order to preserve evidence. At that time we still did not know what condition the victim was but things seemed very grave. The cameras then filmed the briefing led by a Sergeant and my input into it, outlining the risks and what "P" was capable of if he indeed realised the seriousness of what he had done.

We all went to "P's" house and he was arrested with little incident. All I remember him saying is "I don't believe this". He was taken into custody and later charged with GBH, as the victim made it, although suffered a badly broken leg sustained as he fell.

"P" got two years for this offence, which I am sure, was again reduced due to the impact on his family. Funnily enough his wife left him while he was inside, which created another big fuss in the community as she shacked up with another bloke. The victim suffered a broken tibia and fibula and needed a stick to walk afterwards. His injuries were life changing. "P" threw only a single punch over something the victim said he did not like. If only people thought about the potential consequences of their actions before they actioned them. Many a murder has been committed over a single punch.

CHAPTER 11 – DRUGS

The destructive power of drugs runs deeply through society and is a major cause of crime in the community. Drug users, especially those who are addicted to Heroin often resort to crime to fuel their habit. Heroin is relatively cheap. £20 will buy you a bag of heroin, but when users go through 5, 10 or more bags a day if you total it up over a week it soon adds up to a large sum over the months and years. Other recreational drugs also contribute to crime. Cocaine for instance is very fashionable and also affordable. £50 will buy enough to last a weekend, and when combined with alcohol creates a substance in the body called coco ethylene, which can cause people to become agitated and violent.

Despite the fact that drug use was usually a high priority crime among the general public, Police did not put much in the way of resources into it. For sure the bigger dealers were investigated and there were big operations from time to time when sufficient evidence had been collected. One such example was operation Morpheus, which happened just before I became a police officer. It was targeted on the Warden family who had a house in a small village called Begdale, just outside Wisbech. It was a massive operation. Officers travelled to the West Indies undercover and befriended members of the gang before making purchases of drugs from the Warden family. When the warrant itself was executed dozens of officers were involved, including firearms, dogs and the Force Helicopter. Drugs were found everywhere in the fens around the house, buried underground, hidden in socks hanging from trees; everywhere. Almost the whole family was sent to prison for lengthy stretches that varied from three to ten years. It was a major success. The only member of the family,

David Warden was not implicated for simple reason that he was already in prison when the operation was on. More from him later.

This remains the biggest drugs operation ever mounted in the county, and cost a lot of money. The results were fantastic, but of course when the Warden gang was removed others stepped in and took their place. The market was disrupted for a time, but it still carried on. To continually invest the police time and resources into operations such as Morpheus was a non-starter for a small police force such as Cambridgeshire. However on a smaller scale the fight continues, warrants are obtained from court and executed all the time and large finds of cannabis are common. Small amounts of drugs are seized though stop and search and these lead on to bigger finds now and again.

The fight against drugs is very much intelligence led. The police rely heavily on the community to provide the information that is required to go before a magistrate and swear out a warrant. Once police have a warrant the planning can begin in order to raid the address or location concerned. I was a part of dozens of such warrants that were pre-planned operations and I will outline one now.

Wisbech, during the filming of "Cop Squad" by Sky. I was part of a team who executed a warrant issued under the misuse of drugs act at a council house down Southwell Road, which to be fair is not a desirable place to live. The entire operation was filmed on camera, and I had the dubious honour of wearing a Microphone so that everything I said would be recorded.

At 0700 the officer who had organised the operation briefed us. The briefing included the intelligence that led us to the property, the drugs we were looking for, layout of the house and details of probable occupants. All risks were discussed.

I drove a police van to the scene, along with the method of entry team and TV camera. In instances such as this we did not knock politely on the door, as it gave too much time for the occupants to dispose of the evidence. The two-man entry teams role was simple; effect an entry to the house as quickly as possible and then get out of the way to allow officers to enter. The most effective way of achieving this was for the door to be bashed in using an enforcer, basically a big metal battering ram with handles welded to it; otherwise known as the big red key. One officer braces the door in case it is loose in its frame and the other bashes. Normally over in ten seconds or less.

We arrived at the house and I parked up just short. The MOE team ran out to the front door and I followed. A colleague and myself would be the first in the house when entry was gained and we would run straight up the stairs to secure the first floor. The next two officers would follow us but secure the downstairs.

Boom, Boom, Boom, and the door was hanging off its frame. We ran in shouting clearly "Police Officers, no one move". I ran up the stairs and found nothing but filth and dog shit. The upstairs was in a hell of a state and was full of drug paraphernalia such as needles, foil and sharps bins. It stunk of human waste and dog shit.

I went downstairs and found other officers had secured two female occupants whom by this time had both been handcuffed. Two dogs had also been found in an emaciated and dishevelled state. The officer in charge was in the process of explaining to the householder why we were there and showing them the warrant. They made a very quick admission that they had a bit of heroin in their handbag, which they were about to do when we went in. First objective had been met. We had found drugs in the house so the warrant was a success.

An officer looked after the two suspects after they had been searched and the room they were in had been searched too. That way they could remain in that one room that had already been checked. I returned upstairs with a colleague and began searching the upstairs rooms. We were looking for any illegal substances, along with any drug paraphernalia that could be used in the sale of drugs such as bags, scales or large amounts of tin foil. With the amount of rubbish and filth lying around it would be a long job to complete an effective search. So gloves and mask on I began one of the bedrooms. The room had a double bed in it, which was somewhat dirty, and there was no space in the room on the floor to move around. The room was full of dirty clothes, rubbish, and evidence of drug use. There were dirty needles everywhere, on the cupboards, bedside cabinet, under the pillows and on the floor. These needles simply provided the foundations of the crap that lie on top in the form of used silver foil (used for chasing the dragon which is melting the heroin with a lighter and inhaling the fumes) and also discarded wraps which once contained heroin. I found a sharps bin that was crammed full of hundreds of needles as well. I remember showing it to the camera and describing the scene, along with the uses for the foil, citric acids and other items. We had brought along a police drugs dog, which was a lovely black Labrador but I quickly advised the handler that the room was too dangerous for the dog to enter. There were too many sharps. I found nothing of note evidentially, but the council would certainly be interested when the housing officer arrived to speak with the tenant.

A colleague had searched another bedroom and we then moved on to the 'master bedroom' together. The floor was covered in dog shit, but otherwise the room did not show signs of drug use like the other two. We searched the room finding nothing of note and made the mistake of taking our masks off. The sun had been shining through the window and the temperature in the room had risen causing the dog shit of varying freshness to ferment. The result was a gut wrenching stink that caused the both of us to wretch and run downstairs into the front garden. We met various residents of Southwell Road down there watching proceedings that all had a jolly good laugh at our expense.

Upon going back into the house we assisted in the search of the downstairs. There was again needles littered around, but in one case they had been hidden in such a way as to be a booby trap for police. Uncapped needles had been hidden in a vent in the kitchen so when you put your hand in, you would get a needle stick injury. Sinister and not pleasant.

The housing officer arrived and on examining the state of the house advised the tenant that their tenancy was under threat and that they would also be billed for the repair to the door.

The only drugs found were the small amount the householder admitted to when we first gained access. She was interviewed at the house and given a formal caution. On top of that she was evicted from the house by the housing association.

The above tale is an example of a pre-planned operation, but now and again something spontaneous comes up that turns into a major find. Cannabis is still the most widely used illegal substance used in the community. It is cheap to buy and almost everyone knows someone who will sell it to you. However it has to be grown, and the conditions it needs, whilst not exactly being hard to recreate take some effort. These days cannabis is grown right there in the community, with gangs renting out houses, old shops, even old factory units and employing one or two gardeners to grow the crop. These 'Gardeners' are expendable. They are commonly Vietnamese in origin and take all the risks, with themselves possibly victims of people trafficking or even slavery. They live in the house to grow and dry out the crop before it is collected by the dealers and sold on. The risks they face are obviously getting caught by the police as well as being attacked by rival gangs. Most of all these people are valued because they keep their mouths shut when arrested. They are simply in too much fear to speak and are in a foreign country with little or no grasp of British law and the English language.

There was a secluded property out in the countryside, in a location known as the 'Hook', which was on our radar. At the time I was the local officer for the town of Chatteris and I regularly patrolled the area. Occasionally when I passed by I caught the vague whiff of cannabis, which is distinctive. However I could never triangulate it to a particular place. I suspected this property but a high wooden fence, which stopped me from seeing in, surrounded it. A fly over by the Force Helicopter, which used its thermal camera to look for the heat sources that come from the high powered lamps used to cultivate cannabis had turned up nothing of note.

One summer's day a colleague and myself were patrolling the area and on passing the property again caught the all too familiar whiff of cannabis. We stopped and got out of the car. We approached the fence and had a wander around. The smell was very strong and it was obvious that it originated from the property. However we had no power to enter as a smell is not quite enough to enter a premises. We were about to go back to the station and start the paperwork for a warrant when a head appeared over the fence. A young Vietnamese looking chap looked down upon us with a look of pure surprise on his face, before jumping down. We could hear his running footsteps on the gravel in the yard as he ran away. Now, as I could smell the cannabis, and had come onto contact with a person whose response was to flee I had a power to enter under the Police and Criminal Evidence Act. Not thinking I climbed the fence and jumped down the other side.

Wrong move. I was then approached by a previously unseen and very large dog, which looked like a mastiff type. It was about the size of a Rottweiler and was foaming at the mouth as it approached. Several expletives issued forth from my mouth as I pulled out my PAVA spray and pointed it at the dog, thinking that I would have to spray it to stop it attacking me. My colleague had wisely got to the top of the fence and stayed there! The Vietnamese was vaulting the fence at the back and making good his escape over fields.

The dog issued forth a deep growl and it did not look good. I said "Hello Matey" to the dog and tentatively help out my hand to it (but not close enough to be bitten). The dog put its head down and gingerly sniffed my hand before nuzzling it and knocking it to the top of his head so I could scratch behind his ears. Some guard dog, he was as soft as you like! With my colleague now having entered the yard (through an unlocked gate) we approached the property which was a prefabricated bungalow.

The back door was wide open and other officers arrived and began searching the area for the missing gardener. As we went in another male, also Vietnamese was found and detained. He spoke no English and looked terrified. And it was no surprise. Apart from the kitchen, every room, shed and outbuilding were full of cannabis plants in various states of growth. There must have been a total of 500 hundred plants with a street value of nearly a million pounds. This was a decent sized operation.

CID took over the scene and I went out searching for the escaped man, who could not have gone too far in the circumstances. I was in a 4x4 vehicle so drove across a field to the back of the property to begin the search. A police dog had arrived and the handler was just starting a track from the point in the fence the male had left the property from, which was not a high fence. I was a hundred yards away in the 4x4 and would follow at a distance if he picked up a track. Suddenly the Mastiff I found earlier which had been left to roam the garden forced itself through the fence and attacked the police dog, locking its jaws around the scruff of its neck. Police dogs are not shrinking violets and I have seen many a member of the public get growled or snapped at when they approach the nice police doggie! What do they expect? These are working dogs, loved by their handlers and are trained to take people down. They are not there to pet and stroke! However on this occasion the Mastiff had hold and was shaking the police German Shepherd vigorously. The handler had drawn his baton and was hitting the Mastiff repeatedly on its head in an effort to make it release its grip. I began to move forward, because if the dog did not let go, or attacked the handler I would have to run it over and kill it. I did not want to but at the end of the day the Police Dog and the Police Officer with it came first.

The Mastiff let go. It was completely unhurt. The Dog handler grabbed his dog and lifted it quickly into his vehicle. It had been injured but we did not know the severity of it, although its neck was bloody. The Mastiff was not aggressive towards people and a colleague got it on a lead and took it back to the garden.

The Police dog made a full recovery and was not badly hurt. The escaped Vietnamese was never found. The other one said nothing when interviewed and was eventually charged with the cultivation of cannabis. He was not treated harshly and was deported. The cannabis itself was ripped out of its pots and bagged up to be incinerated. All the equipment was seized and destroyed also. This was a major find, and just goes to show what you can turn up simply by mooching around. The argument the government makes about visible presence and the value of patrol being not so important now is shown to be rubbish by this incident.

Stop and Search is also a valuable tool in the fight against crime in general, as well as combating drug dealers and users. A single stop can reveal many things and lead police to other searches at the person's home address. When someone is taken into custody for an offence, be it possession or possession with intent to supply the duty inspector can be approached for the authorisation of a Section 18 search. This empowers the police to attend the address of the suspect and conduct a search there for more drugs, or in the case of the arrest being for theft-stolen property.

Of all the tools police have, stop and search is one of the most effective. Providing you have the grounds to stop and search a person you can find anything. And having the grounds to search is the most important thing. You may not have any grounds at all when you come across someone, but their behaviour and attitude may well lead an officer to become suspicious. Also if you see someone who is a known burglar, drug user or dealer etc in the right conditions it is wholly appropriate to 'spin' them as I called it. Before you can search a person you must have several things in place, which is encompassed in an acronym ' GO WISELY.' You have to go through this procedure every time you search someone and also record the search on a form of which the person is entitled a copy of on the spot, or at any time six months later. I will go through it quickly now:

G – Give your grounds for the search.

O – Object of the search. What you are looking for.

W – Warrant card. If you are not in uniform show your warrant card.

I – Identify Yourself. Give your Rank and Collar Number.

S – Station. What station you are from.

E – Entitled. Person is entitled to a copy of the form.

L – Legal Power. Explain the legal power you are using.

Y – You. You are detained for the duration of the search.

It is important for everyone to know the above information. Most searches completed by police officers are perfectly legal, but for a variety of reasons the law can be bent and changed to suit a situation. I used Stop and Search powers on countless occasions and in my view never once abused the power, but the law can be applied in many different ways and if you have been stopped and searched, without the above then the officer who stopped you has done wrong and you should report it.

With regard to Drug use again, the subject of this chapter. I once stopped a young man in the early hours of the morning who was riding a bike. He was acting furtively, in that he was staying in the shadows and was wearing a hooded top with the hood covering his face. He had also cycled across the road in front of my police vehicle causing me to brake sharply. I recognised him from a photograph in briefing that stated that he might be involved in car crime and burglary. I therefore searched him as per the above for stolen items or items he could use to commit burglary. I found nothing in regard to that, but did find a small amount of cannabis on him. This meant little in itself. I would seize the cannabis and issue him a warning, but he rather dropped himself in it by saying "I have three nine bars at home" A 'nine bar' is a nine ounce block of cannabis resin. Resin is different from herbal cannabis or skunk as it is called now, as it is a solid block of material refined from cannabis. It is not really in fashion now and is not seen much as it is not as potent as skunk and is harder to make.

Three nine bars was a significant amount, worth about £700, and was enough to justify a charge of possession with intent to supply.

Within Section 18 of the Police And Criminal Evidence Act (PACE) there is a provision to self-authorise a Section 18 search of someone's home if it is necessary to do it quickly, and for the detained person to be there. It is called a Section 18 (5) search. I decided to do this on this occasion (but still contacted the duty Inspector to make sure it was ok). Accompanied by my Sergeant I went to the detainee's address and he gave us the three bars of cannabis resin. He was arrested further for possession with intent to supply and we took him through to custody for interview. During the interview he would not tell us where he got it from (of course) but did say he had been given it to sell for a fee. It was not his, and he would now be in a lot of trouble with the dealer as he had lost it. I got the impression that he did not want it and took this chance to get rid of it without getting a kicking but he really was not the sharpest tool in the box. He was charged and went to court in the end.

The lad did not go to prison and as it was his first offence he got handed a community sentence. He obviously did not learn his lesson, or the dealer made him work off the debt by selling more drugs as he was caught again. He ended up leaving the area to escape the people he now owed money to. This is not a glamorous or particularly exciting story but it does highlight the value of good old-fashioned police work, patrolling and turning things up yourself. More often than not these days officers are too busy to do this and instead are chasing their tales being slaves to the radio. Being proactive in this manner reduces crime and makes the community feel safer, something that cannot be bought and increases public faith in the service.

Recent cuts over the last five years mean that there are not enough bobbies out there to fulfil calls for service and the skill of self-generating work is disappearing.

CHAPTER 12– THEFT AND BURGLARY

If you have been the victim of burglary you will know how it feels. It is simply horrible knowing that someone has been in your home and gone through your things, looking for valuables and just taking things you have worked hard to own or had passed to you by relatives that are no longer with us. It is such an invasion of privacy that many people feel they have to move house to escape the feeling of intrusion. Burglary is a crime that you can take steps to avoid, but more often than not burglars are seldom caught at the scene and if they are in the slightest bit forensically aware rarely caught at all.

As a Police Officer it is very tough to sit in someone's front room, that has been trashed and go through the items that have been stolen with them. With the elderly it is particularly tough and can sometimes mean the end of their being able to live independently in their own home.

There is little the initial police officer can do to catch the criminals responsible at that point. In most cases when Burglaries are detected it is through fingerprints or other forensic evidence such as DNA through blood or a discarded cigarette. I always made a point however of closely examining the scene, establishing the entry and exit points and trying to identify points of interest for the CSI (Crime scene investigator). I would at least make an effort to let the victim know I was taking it seriously, but faith was often so low that the victim already believed they had seen the last of their possessions. We would leave the victim to sit in the mess that had been made of their house, not even being able to repair broken windows or doors until CSI had attended.

There are more impactful burglaries, which actually change definition to Robbery or Aggravated burglary. This is when the offenders will burst in when the victim is at home and offer violence, for example tying up victims and beating them or using threats of violence. There have been cases involving the elderly where they have been confronted by or disturbed burglars that have become murder enquiries.

One such example I attended was a case of Robbery. A local man I will refer to as "F", lived alone in a very small flat located on the top floor of a block in the centre of March. He made his living buying and selling gold coins and medallions. He kept himself to himself and was not involved in any crime that Police were aware of.

I was called to the flat one afternoon, the Robbery had happened in broad daylight. I found "F" battered, beaten and bruised curled up in a ball on the floor. The door had been kicked in.

A gang of four men had crashed into the flat and grabbed him, beating him senseless. They knew what he did and that he would have gold coins amongst other valuables in the flat. They had beaten him already, but then proceeded to trash the flat looking for items to steal. Finding nothing they then held "F's" fingers between garden shears and began cutting his fingers off.

"F" had not lost any fingers, and the gang left empty handed. However he had been severely beaten and shaken. Funnily enough he would not make a complaint or make a statement to the police, which of course aroused everyone's suspicions. He went off to hospital and nothing else was said on the matter. A crime was raised and filed immediately undetected.

The police never got to the bottom of this incident. I am sure that he owed money to someone, or had been caught out doing something he should not have. All we knew of the gang that attacked him was that they were eastern European. Nothing else was said and we got nowhere.

CHAPTER 13 – BRAIN WORMS AND TEARS

I have talked about mental health and its effects. I have tried to be objective and show that it is real, and kills hundreds of people every year. But I never thought it would affect me. I was a Copper, experienced and resilient, I was indestructible.

In fact I had been suffering from a mental illness in silence and alone for years. Ever since the Halloween RTC outlined earlier, and compounded by the tragic death of Charlotte in the 16 foot River the following February. I managed this illness myself, and the ups and downs that came with it for another 5 years before I sought any help, and by then it was too late to save my career, which I loved.

Soon after the October RTC I began to have flash backs. These were vivid and disturbing as I relived the events of the incident time and time again. I would revisit each part of the incident, including sounds and smells and the flashbacks would come every time my mind was at rest. I would be washing up, and would suddenly realise I was in tears. Time had simply stood still while my mind tormented me. I had periods where I would have 20 or 30 of these events each day. They would happen whilst driving and I would be unable to recollect how I have negotiated a roundabout, or why I was upset and crying (again). I was having these the following February at the 16 Foot when I was manning a road closure. And afterwards this RTC joined in too. I would subconsciously avoid driving near any water, going miles out of my way and not realising it. My mental health deteriorated and at times I was pretty much unapproachable by anyone apart from my kids and girlfriend, (now wife) Claire. I was moody, sad and unable to motivate myself at all. My performance at work ran in peaks of high performance and then dips where I was just not interested. Eventually in

2012 I was put on an action plan and transferred to Wisbech from NPT so I could be closely supervised. I did not breath a word of how I was feeling to anyone.

At times I was OK. Flashbacks did not happen as much and I was able to focus on home life as well as work. But then they would come back it would all return. At times I was manic, performing brilliantly as a response officer, receiving compliments and good work reports from colleagues and quickly passing my action plan. But I could not sustain it. Mistakes began to slip in that I was completely oblivious of. However my colleagues on shift continued to support me and I thought respected me.

One such colleague did not. A local Sergeant had taken a dislike to me. We just did not get on, and our approaches to policing were poles apart. He was of the old school; nick everyone and sort everything out later. I was more reserved and used my power of arrest sparingly, using other approaches such as restorative justice to achieve what I felt were fairer and more effective results. The sergeant began scrutinising and complaining about almost everything I did. He was always in the ear of my shift inspector and sergeant making comments that they ignored to the most part. I knew it was bullying but I did not want to complain. At the end of the day he was still a brother officer. Also I had complained before, writing a full report to my Inspector a couple of years before which resulted only in my being moved stations, the bullying continuing. I had spoken with my shift Sergeant regarding the issue and had been encouraged that I had a good case. I wish I had taken it further.

On the 31st October 2012 (I know Halloween again) I was on an early shift. I was surprised to be called into the duty Inspectors office straight after briefing. He normally worked over the Huntingdon end so it was weird that he was even there.

It was horrible. I was served with a Reg 9 notice containing 5 allegations made against me. These allegations regarded three crimes I had detected and dealt with the offender using Restorative Justice. Also under investigation were a Fixed Penalty Notice I had issued to a shoplifter and two stop searches I have performed a month or so earlier. I will summarise the allegations below.

1. I had failed to hand over a £45 donation to charity to a local supermarket handed to me by a shoplifting offender as compensation for shoplifting.

2. I had failed to hand over £5.00 to a local shop as compensation for shoplifting.

3. I had not dealt with a shoplifting incident quickly enough which was being dealt with by way of Restorative Justice.

4. I had issued forms for stop searches on two occasions which had not taken place, and that these were false records.

I was dismayed. 1, and 2 above were both allegations that would result in criminal charges and dismissal if proven. I was confident that they would not be as I certainly knew that in one case the monies had been handed over, and in one instance never received. And the other allegations were just rubbish frankly. I told the Inspector as such. He then handed me a note from the Chief Inspector stating that I was removed from the evidential chain and I could have nothing to do with any form of crime or front line police work. That got me. I was on the verge of tears from that point. Demeaningly I then had to be escorted to my locker where all my kit was searched. They took all the paperwork in there, and most of my past pocket note books. However nothing was found supporting any of the allegations. I was told I was going to be sent to work in the crime unit in Peterborough where I would be filing crime folders. I was already feeling low as the flashbacks had been back for a month or two and the depression was setting in as well. I went off to the toilet and phoned Claire, having five minutes or so of sobbing and being generally hysterical.

I saw my shift colleagues briefly and to be fair my shift Sergeant was great. There was nothing for me to do there at that moment so I went home, and awaited being advised when I was to start at CMU, which turned out to be the following day.

I lasted a few days at CMU. The work was so boring and monotonous I could not stand it. The lack of stimulation just let the flashbacks in and I could not deal with it, I went home in a blind panic and Claire came with me to see the doctor.

What came next was a blur. I told the doctor everything that was going in with my head, and for the first time admitted that I had regularly contemplated suicide. The Doctor was fantastic. He put me in touch with the crisis team, referred me for further treatment and counselling and prescribed medication to help me raise my mood. It would take time to work but the sooner I started the better. But most of all the person I have to thank is my wife Claire. She was my tower of strength, my guide and my love. She helped me see that even though I was ill there was a way through it. She wanted me to stay busy, keep my mind focussed and above all do not do anything daft.

I was off work for a total of 3 months. While I was off I started to have treatment which started with Cognitive Behavioural Therapy and counselling which did nothing for me, as well as several visits to my GP where the dosage of medication I was taking went up to the maximum I could have. I was still having flashbacks and the medication made me sluggish, uninterested and to be honest not all there.

This did not stop PSD. I was called in for interview I believe on three occasions during the time I was ill. These were criminal interviews as well as those regarding conduct. I was accompanied by a federation representative and a solicitor. They all thought it was total bullshit. I felt that it was wrong to be interviewing me while I was sick and not all there to be honest but I was told if I did not submit to voluntary interview I would be arrested and dealt with in custody. I should have complained but it all washed over me.

However the stress of the investigation helped little and I returned to thinking about suicide again. I worked out how to do it using my car and Carbon Monoxide poisoning. I found a length of hose that fitted around the exhaust of my old car and was just the right length to reach the passenger rear window. I planned when it would happen and where. I was only stopped by my car running out of petrol.. sad or what?

I was referred to a Psychiatrist who I began to have sessions with. I had hardly heard of PTSD and when I was diagnosed I was happy that what was haunting me had a name at last. Even this made me feel a bit better.

An old Inspector had moved to the Peterborough area and had started a project with Cambridge University criminology department. He had asked for an officer to help out with this and my name was mentioned. He was happy to have me. During my sickness review I was asked if I felt ready for a phased return to work and to help with this project. I jumped at it. I spent the next three months with this project, completing a valuable piece of work and feeling valued again. I even heard rumours that the Divisional Superintendent wanted to use me on another project after my disciplinary was over and keep me in the division. I began to feel that I was going to be ok. This was reinforced that the decision maker had decided that there were to be no criminal charges brought against me for thefts of the money mentioned earlier.

My Disciplinary was scheduled for the 12th and 13th June 2013. During the hearing I was to be supported by a federation representative and a Barrister. The Barrister had a very impressive name, Gerrard Pounder and I felt confident that such an eminent

member of the Barr would live up to their name.

CHAPTER 14 – NO ONE CARES. NO ONES LISTENING.

Before I go on to talk about the hearing that eventually saw me out on my ear as a Copper, I want to share with you what I said in all the interviews and how I responded to the allegations. Firstly I was contrite, self-deprecating and honest in everything I said. If I had done something wrong I said so straight away. This was what I had been told to do. The message from the Chief Constable at the time was for all officers to use their professional judgement, be prepared to justify your actions, and if a mistake had been made in good faith it would be seen as a learning opportunity. I made no effort to excuse or hide anything I did wrong and like an idiot I made no mention of my mental illness as a reason my performance was poor when the reality was that my mental illness was the whole reason why my performance was poor as well as at times; excellent. The interview process was horrible. Obviously they started with criminal interviews (which I participated in voluntarily) so they could deal with the alleged theft of the £45 compensation from the shoplifting. After this they dealt with the other matters as misconduct. I had a solicitor and a federation representative with me for each interview. As I have mentioned before there was no consideration that I was fit for interview due to my mental health, and on one occasion there was mock concern when I disclosed that I had suicidal thoughts with both investigators saying "Ohhhhh don't tell us that! In a mocking manner. Looking back this makes me want to vomit. I was even told that this would not result in my losing my job at on stage (off record) with the investigator telling me that if they thought that I would be given the discharger papers to sign, and they were not considering that. I was not myself and said a lot of things that made me look terrible, that anyone in their right state of mind would not have done.

The matter of the £45.00 missing from the settlement of a restorative justice case was the sole reason for my dismissal. The reason why was that the PSD alleged that I had indeed stolen it which was not the case. What happened was this. I was sent to a shoplifting incident in a well-known Supermarket in Wisbech. The offender was a middle-aged woman who had no previous convictions and had led a careful, crime free life. She fully admitted what she had done and expressed remorse as well as obviously feeling a great deal of shame and embarrassment. It was a one-off error of judgement, triggered by a mental health illness. I decided that restorative justice would be perfect in that this was a way of making reparation for the crime, without the offender obtaining a criminal record. The offender and victim (Supermarket) agreed and the resolution was authorised by my Sergeant. The offender agreed to pay £45.00 in compensation and also write a letter of apology. I left the scene and the crime was raised and detected.

After a day or two I was sent an envelope containing the money and also the letter. At this time, I put it in my tray ready for me to drop off at the supermarket. What I failed to do was book the envelope into the property system. I thought I would be able to drop the envelope off in a day or two saving me this small administration task. Idiot. Very quickly a couple of weeks went by. I had taken it out on patrol with me several times meaning to drop it off but been diverted to emergency incidents each time. I always returned it to my tray at the end of the shift. Finally, on a late night shift an "A" grade incident came in at the supermarket and I attended with my partner for the night. As we were in the station at the time of the call, I grabbed the envelope to hand over whilst there.

The incident was another shoplifting committed by a very drunk and abusive foreign national. We quickly had him arrested and cuffed, sat in a chair and being quiet.

Whilst chatting to the security staff I took the letter and cash from my pouch and removed it from the envelope, handing it to the store detective. I never thought another thing about it. My fundamental error was not to get a receipt signed in my pocket notebook by the store detective acknowledging receipt of the letter and money. Having said that the store detective was the same one who dealt with the original shoplifting incident and remembered – surely if the money was no longer with the letter (I had secured them with a paper clip) they would have asked.

Anyway, we went off with our prisoner and dealing with him ended up taking the rest of the shift. I never thought anything else about the matter until months later I received the Reg 15 notice from the Inspector. What I was absolutely clear about was that to the best of my knowledge the money was handed over, I never saw it again and I did not take it. I did not need this money as I earned a good salary as an officer and in addition my wife and I had been gifted a large sum of money by a relative. We were about to go on an expensive holiday. How anyone thought that I would have taken this money was beyond me.

PSD were like a dog with a bone. There was CCTV showing me handing over the letter and it did not show me acting suspiciously or furtively. My colleague also gave a statement saying he had seen me handing something over (but was not aware as to what). They went as far as to get an envelope, write a letter and fasten £45 to it with a paperclip and simulate how hard it was to separate the two, insinuating that I must have known. This was done as I had suggested that the money could have come loose from the paperclip and had been left in the envelope, which I had disposed of. The reason it was disposed of was that after attending a really nasty sudden death myself and my colleague attending were infested with fleas. I had to go home, remove all my uniform and everything in my pockets and chuck them all away. This included the envelope that went into the bin along with all my traffic paperwork and tickets. I was the first to admit that this was a ridiculous hypothesis, but it was the only explanation I could think of, particularly in my mental state. The truth of the matter was that if I had followed the correct procedures in booking the letter and cash into property and getting a receipt, I would never have been in this position to begin with. I had not solen the money but admitted that I was guilty of not following the right protocols. I refused to accuse the store detective of taking the money and took it on myself, with the insistence that I did not take it. PSD tried to get a criminal conviction and submitted a file in order to have me prosecuted for theft, but the Chief Superintendent refused to proceed through the non-existence of any evidence.

So, there was no criminal prosecution coming which went a long way to make me feel better and imagine being able to resume my career after the disciplinary hearing. However I was told that the incident was still being dealt with as gross misconduct which meant that my job was still on the line.

The other matters facing me were to do with another incident of Restorative justice, where there had been a theft of some children's shoes from a local business park. The store had managed to get the registration number of the car used to commit the theft and I was allocated the crime. I went to the address given by PNC (Police National Computer) and found a mother and her young daughter. They had no money and mum had stolen the shoes as her daughter was being bullied at school. She fully admitted the offence. I proposed Restorative Justice as the mother had no criminal convictions and showed remorse, as well as making a full and frank admission to the theft. PSD asserted that I had not dealt with this case quickly enough. This was just plain ridiculous as I had only had the crime allocated to me a week and had already traced and dealt with the offender. Eventually it was dropped. I am mentioning it here as I want to show that the PSD were hell bent on nailing me with absolutely anything they could find.

The last matters I had to answer for were Stop and Searches. Police in the UK have the power to stop and ask someone to account for their presence in a public place, and if certain conditions are met can also search them for certain objects. These included drugs, weapons or items used to commit burglary. The Force were extremely keen on sing stop and search as it led to a lot of convictions which meant in turn detected crimes, making the figures look better. Every month every officer had to produce the numbers of stop/search they had completed that month along with many other statistics such as traffic process, incidents attended and arrests. I always did well in this "performance indicators" and often was near the top. Officers with consistently lower figures were asked to explain why. There was pressure to perform.

The first incident concerned a load of kids we had caught drinking alcohol in a school playground late one night. I had taken the names and addresses of all the young people and was arranging to have a letter sent to their parents to ensure they were advised what their little darlings were up to. In order to do this each young person had to have a stop search form with a box ticked for the Guardian Awareness Programme. I believe I did five of them. I commented to my partner that all the forms would make our stats look good. I did not do the forms at the time but advised each person that a form will be available at the police station for them should a parent wish to see it. PSD maintained that all the forms should have been done there and then and the people each given their copies. I maintained that as I had advised that a copy was available at the police station what I had done was acceptable. I had urgent tasks to complete for the Inspector that night and did not want to be delayed. I was found guilty of breaching the standards of professional conduct at my hearing for this. I though it absolutely ridiculous and petty.

The second incident related to an almost identical incident. I was on patrol on my own late at night and came across to men in a secluded alleyway. It was a known area for drugs, so I stopped the two males and asked them to account for their whereabouts. This technically according to my training constituted a stop search so I completed stop search forms. I did these at the station as I did not feel it safe to be filling out forms late at night, with no backup with two males who were acting suspiciously. PSD alleged that I had never seen these men and the stop search records were false. However, the males were found and reported that they had spoken with me and I had been most courteous. Undeterred PSD changed the goal posts and went after me again for not filling in the form at the time of the stops despite my asserting it was not safe to do so. I was done for that too. Final written warning for following my training. When I got to the hearing, with the Assistant Chief Constable chairing, along with two other high ranking officers on the board everyone took an hour saying how the whole process was about finding out the truth, there would be no trick questions and it would be conducted fairly and impartially. What a load of bollocks. I have never before, or since seen such a loaded situation. PSD presented the evidence and I was questioned by the panel and the PSD inspector presenting the case. By questioned I meant cross examined – they asked me question after question, looking for ways to trip me up or expose me as careless/dishonest or whatever. My barrister protested that I was ill and suffering from a mental health disorder, taking strong medication and was a disorganised officer, borne from years of suffering from a mental health disorder; not a dishonest one. It was to no avail. Despite supporting statements from colleagues stating I am not dishonest, and a hundred or so good work emails from superiors over the years. After two days they found me guilty of gross misconduct and dismissed me from the service without so much as a backward glance. They did not accept any mitigation in the form of my PTSD and the fact that it had almost killed me. All I got was a statement "we appreciate how upsetting the two RTC were". Looking back, I still wrankle at the unfairness of it. I loved being a copper. It was everything I was, or at least I felt it was. My hearing was conducted like a criminal trial and I think the end result was pre-ordained. It was a sham.

Even now, I think of all the friends who advised me to sue the force for the mishandling of my mental health following the incidents that caused my illness. I have read of officers doing the same and receiving six figure pay-outs; one such officer suing the force as their riot training frightened them and caused PTSD. Every now and again I think back and wish I had tried it, for the financial settlement alone to ensure my families security. This is short lived. They sacked me as they said they found it impossible to believe I had left that supermarket not knowing I still had the £45.00 on me and basically said I had nicked it. This is not what happened, but I did fuck it up. At the end of the day the reason I am not a copper now is the mistakes I made. I don't think it would have been fair to sue the police force as for me, it would have been for revenge.

I drove home in a daze and collapsed into Claire's arms. For days I did not want anyone around me other than her, but the force decided to cause more upset by sending a Sergeant round for my uniform the following morning… nice and sensitive.

CHAPTER 14 – EPILOGUE

The day after my dismissal I started the process of re-entry into the real world, as well as ongoing treatment for my mental health illness. Socially coppers always stick together and most of my mates were police officers or staff. Only Pasty really stuck with me. I had a text from my Shift Sergeant saying she was in tears after finding out what happened, and my shift colleagues were upset too. This was nice, but as I had heard nothing from any of them the whole time the investigation went on (four months) I found it a bit hard to believe. I was not resentful as this is what always happened with PSD. Colleagues were told not to contacted me. I had seen it happen time and time again. Targets were isolated so they could not turn to anyone for support.

I went and claimed Jobseekers as it was then and found I was also entitled to Housing Benefit. The Jobseekers was withdrawn as I had been dismissed which was classed as deliberately making myself unemployed which was super (Thank you Mr Cameron). I did not mean to be unemployed long, however.

As an ex police officer with a lot of training and specialisms I was confident I would walk into any job of my choosing. This was not the case as I received knockback after knockback. I was given no reasons other than I had just been pipped by someone else who had either more experience or came across just that little bit better in interview. Claire and I began to look for a smaller house as we could no longer afford the one, we lived in. Eventually I found work as a traffic warden, earning minimum wage, and from there I have flitted from job to job never staying anywhere long. I have not been able to settle and have never been able to earn as much as I had as a police officer until a year ago.

It is now 2020 and I have just been offered a job as the manager of a children's home with a salary of nearly 40K per annum. This is roughly what I would have been on now had I still been a Bobby. Over the time since leaving the police I have struggled severely financially but had spent seven glorious years married to my soul mate Claire.

It has taken me seven years to write this journal. Part of the reasons why have been motivation, and not wanting to relive any of the significant events documented over the course of my tale. Also, I have not wanted to talk about my issues, and how I finally conquered PTSD.

I went through therapy for around 18 months. PTSD is an issue with the part of your brain which deals with memories. Traumatic events in your life go through stages as your brain processes them, leading eventually to the memories being stored in the long-term area of your brain. PTSD is an issue where this long-term filing of memories fails and the sufferer remains with them in the short term memory and relives them time and time again.

To address this, I underwent several sessions of Eye Movement Desensitisation Therapy (EMDR). Studies had shown that creating eye movement whilst re living the traumatic memories hoodwinks the brain into refiling the memory long term. The eye movement is caused by flashing lights that alternate between the left and right eye. As this goes on you talk about and describe the events. The therapy was exhausting and lengthy but eventually it started working and I found myself suffering fewer and then zero flashbacks. It took 18 months. It did not stop the anxiety and depression which continued for more years but eventually I also got a handle on that by positive thinking and finding my love of performing.

My daughter Olivia was and is a budding actor. She appeared as one of Fagin's gang in Oliver with Spalding Amateur Dramatic and Operatic Society (SADOS) and I was persuaded to audition for their next production – The Games Afoot. Surprisingly I was offered a part and the fun, discipline of rehearsal and appearing on stage in a real theatre as given me a joy and focus I will never give up. I have made so many friends and now acting is the most important thing in my life apart from family. I have even done Shakespeare! I have even tried my hand at directing (the show was great but the tole on my mental health made my own behaviour embarrassing). Where I am now is a happy place. I feel fulfilled professionally and I am so happy with my darling wife Claire. My kids are nearly all grown up with one studying Law at Warwick, one having her GCSE results today (which were excellent) and my 15-year-old stepdaughter who has her challenges but still makes me proud. I love them all and this book is for them.

Finally, what have I learned? Honesty is still the best policy, especially to one's self. Had I admitted to myself I was in trouble all those years ago and sought the help I needed the last decade would have been very different, although I do not know I would have been happier today. It is ok to admit weakness, seek advice or feel afraid. It is normal to make mistakes, you just need to recognise and learn from them and always strive to be better moving forward. Treat people well and to use a current phrase – Be kind.

My reasons for writing this work are mainly to show to myself that I once was a good police officer and to heal myself of the shame I felt when I was sacked from the job I loved and was so proud of. I am still proud, and my achievements and mistakes make me who I am today. I am still learning and still making mistakes. I hope it continues.

I am not bitter. The British Police are the best police force in the world. They run towards the danger others flee from every day and Police Officers up and down the country are killed every day protecting us. They do this by consent, largely without guns or other lethal equipment. As a result they remain respected and loved by the public. I remain proud to have served, and still prouder of my colleagues past present and future who will all remain part of the police family.

Printed in Great Britain
by Amazon